Dedicated
to the pastor and friends
who encouraged me
to investigate

Introduction

There are three chief records that tell the story of the human race.

Until now the three records have never been integrated into a comprehensible whole. This book does just that. Here for the first time is a book that tells how astrology, archaeology, and Bible prophecy interrelate to tell the complete story of mankind.

The three records do not compete with each other, nor do they contradict each other. They explain and support each other.

The first record is the parade of the astrological ages, which are succeeding eras one after another of about 2000 years each. They make up the Great Year in astrology. Each of the astrological ages is a month of the Great Year. We are now living in the Age of Pisces, and according to the signs of the times around us we are nearing the end of it.

The second record has been found in the ground, unearthed by the archaeologists. It is the progression of the anthropological ages from the Ice Ages, through the Stone Ages, the Bonze Ages, and the Iron Ages. They are followed by the industrial age and the space age. Every archaeological dig reveals another piece of the picture of how people have lived on earth.

The third record is the account of the human family as told in the Bible, the epochs of which were all foretold before they happened. The present time – as never before – fairly explodes with the unfolding of the fulfillment of Bible prophecy. The Bible recounts the events of the anthropological ages. The archaeologists continually anthropological ages. The archaeologists continually uncover evidence that confirms the biblical record. The Bible supports the principles of astrology as part of the clockwork of the universe.

The corruptions attached to astrology through the ages have no place in this book. Nor is there room for the misuses people have tried to make of astrology, or for the misconceptions that people have assumed. Astrology is confirmed here as it was created and ordained.

The author has visited and photographed many of the historical and biblical sites written about in the book. Fran Fielden has a Master of Arts in Teaching degree from Winthrop University. An educator, author, and scholar, she is listed in *Who's Who in the South and Southwest* and in *Who's Who of American Women.* As a Bible teacher and a student of astrology for many years, she sees no conflict between the two.

All three of the records – astrology, anthropology, and Bible prophecy – merge with one another in this book. Their intertwining is its thesis. All three records are currently vital and relevant. *Astrology and Prophecy* relates them to our lives and expectations.

Contents

"...I know the thoughts and plans that I
have toward you, says the Lord,
thoughts and plans of peace
and not of evil,
to give you a future
and a hope."

(Jeremiah 29:11)

Chapter 1

Prophets and Seers

There are questions which come to one's mind about prophecy.

Can people really predict the future?
Is there a time barrier, similar to the sound barrier, which can be broken?
Is the future predicted in the Bible?
When is prophecy the real thing?
Can psychics predict the future?
Is it all right to want to know what is going to happen?
Are there prophets today as in Bible times?
Is the fulfillment of prophecy inevitable?
Why study Bible prophecy?
And add to these questions, what has astrology to do with prophecy?

This book will answer these questions and more.

The word "prophecy" wears many faces. The most authentic of these is Bible prophecy. Throughout the Scriptures God has always informed His people about what was going to happen. *"Surely the Lord God does nothing, unless He reveals His secret to His servants, the prophets"* (Amos 3:7). *"Now I tell you before it comes, that when it does come to pass, you may believe..."* (John 13:19).

True and False Prophets

There have been many who have tried unsuccessfully to emulate the true prophets. The Law of Moses had a remedy for getting rid of these. The fraudulent claimants were put to death. The test they had to pass was whether or not their prophecies were fulfilled. *"But the prophet who presumes to speak a word in My name, which I have not commanded him to speak, or who speaks in the name of other gods, that prophet shall die"* (Deuteronomy 18:20). And die they did, by stoning.

Prophecy is a message that breaks the time barrier. It is a phenomenon that fascinates the human mind. Therefore, there have always been deceiving persons speaking in the name of prophecy who have said what people wanted to hear. It was true in the days of Jeremiah. *"An astonishing and horrible thing has been committed in the land: the prophets prophesy falsely...and My people love to have it so..."* (Jeremiah 5:31).

There will always be a prevalence of false prophets. Jesus, when speaking of the last days of this age, said, *"Then many false prophets will rise up and deceive many"* (Matthew 24:11).

At the same time there have been and always will be the true prophets to whom the Lord has spoken. The apostle Paul wrote about the genuine foreseers of the future. *"Now there are diversities of gifts...for to some is given the gift of prophecy..."* (1 Corinthians 12:4,10). *"Having then gifts differing according to the grace that is given to us, let us use them: if prophecy, let us prophesy in proportion to our faith"* (Romans 12:6).

The apostle John was one of those true prophets. John,

the writer of the book of Revelation, saw a vision of Jesus Christ who said to him, *"'Write the things which you have seen, and the things which are, and the things which will take place after this'"* (Revelation 1:19).

Two Kinds of Angels

There are two kinds of supernatural beings at work in the world today. There are demons, or fallen angels, and there are the angels of God. Both groups can appear to people. Some from each category make predictions of the future.

One of these appears in a story in the New Testament about a slave girl who was possessed by a spirit of divination. The Apostle Paul, annoyed by her constantly following him about, cast out the demon of divination. The girl, whole again, ceased her fortune-telling, much to the distress of her profit-making owners (Acts 16).

The girl had been possessed by an entity who could make supernatural revelations. The fallen angels, or demons, can do this. These angels are distinct from the good angels of God. The differences in the two groups must be understood.

Fallen angels are the henchmen of the devil. When Satan was cast out of heaven because as an angel of high authority he sought to put himself above God, the angels who had aligned themselves with him were also cast out. The Bible says that the fallen ones comprised one-third of the angelic population of heaven. Jesus described the exodus: *"I saw Satan fall like lightning from heaven"* (Luke 10:18).

Cast down from heaven, the activity of demons is to

deceive and destroy. They can mimic people who have lived and died. They pose as channelers, teachers, and masters. Contrary to their true nature, they often appear as angels of light. They hate the name of Jesus Christ, the Son of God. They deny His divinity.

In contrast, the angels of God are those who never lost their exalted position in heaven. They are the servants of God's people, from guardian angels to comforting spirits. *"Are not the angels all ministering spirits, sent out in the service of those who are to inherit salvation?"* (Hebrews 1:14).

Both groups of angels inhabit the air and interact with people. The good angels worship God, assist, protect, and deliver His people. The evil angels oppose God and try to thwart His plans.

Balaam was a prophet in the Old Testament who formerly used sorcery, a method of foretelling the future with the aid of evil spirits. After an experience with the true Spirit of God, Balaam prophesied only the words of the Lord. *"Now when Balaam saw that it pleased the Lord to bless Israel, he did not go as at other times, to seek to use sorcery, but Balaam said, 'Though Balak (the king of Moab) were to give me his house full of silver and gold, I could not go beyond the word of the Lord...what the Lord says, that I must speak'"* (Numbers 24:1,12,13).

Then Balaam spoke the beautiful prophetic words about the Messiah who would come fourteen centuries later:

> *"I see Him, but not now:*
> *I behold him, but not near;*
> *A star shall come out of Jacob;*
> *A Scepter shall rise out of Israel..."*
>
> (Numbers 24:17)

Some of the most beloved stories in the Bible are about angels who appeared as messengers of God. One of these tells of Gabriel, the angel who appeared to Mary of Nazareth to tell her that she would give birth to Jesus, the Son of God. *"...The angel Gabriel was sent by God....and said to Mary, 'You will...bring forth a Son and shall call His name Jesus. He will be great, and will be called the Son of the Highest...'"* (Luke 1:26,31).

At the time of Jesus' birth angels appeared to shepherds in the fields. One said *"I bring you good tidings of great joy which shall be to all people. For there is born a Savior, who is Christ the Lord....Glory to God in the highest, and on earth peace to people of good will!"* (Luke 2:10,11,14).

How does one distinguish between the angels of God and the angels who fell from heaven and became demons? They both appear to people as beings of enlightenment, but there is a difference. The distinguishing factor lies in their message concerning Jesus Christ. If angels hail Jesus as the Son of God, they are angels of God. If the spirit entities describe Jesus as an equal with many other teachers – Buddha, Mohammed, and others – those spirits are fallen demons and not from God.

"For many deceivers have gone out into the world who do not confess Jesus Christ as coming in the flesh. This is a deceiver and an antichrist" (2 John 7). *"Beloved, do not believe every spirit, but test the spirits, whether they are of God; because many false prophets have gone out into the world....Every spirit that confesses that Jesus Christ has come in the flesh is of God, and every spirit that does not confess that Jesus Christ has come in the flesh is not of God..."* (1 John 4:1-3). So there is a way to test spirits, channelers,

masters, and all the rest of unearthly advisers.

A Potpourri of Prophets

Outside the Scriptures, many have come in the name of prophecy. Edgar Cayce was an American prophet who lived from 1877 to 1945. He received and related his messages, including accurate medical diagnoses, while in a trance. His words and predictions were recorded by others, and when he awoke he remembered nothing of what he had said. Years before it happened, he foretold the stock market crash of 1929. In 1931 he envisioned World War II. He predicted great seismic movements under the earth's crust which were to occur from 1958 to 1998. Cayce was a believer in the Bible and at times was greatly baffled by his psychic gift.

Outside the Bible also, two seers who prophesied – the Frenchman Michael Nostradamus and American Jeane Dixon – have captured the public's interest and curiosity. These two were believers in the Scriptures, and both considered their talent of foretelling the future to be a gift from God. Neither claimed to be a prophet of God in the Old Testament sense. Neither was infallible. Both were astrologers.

Both Nostradamus and Dixon made many predictions which parallel certain Bible prophecies.

Michael Nostradamus

Our chief interest here is in Nostradamus as a prognosticator. Some knowledge of Nostradamus the man, however, is necessary to our understanding of Nostradamus the prophet.

Michel de Nostredame, better known by his Latin name, Nostradamus, was born almost 500 years ago. He was a true Renaissance man, exemplifying the revival of learning of the period. Born in St. Remy de Provence on December 23, 1503 (Gregorian Calendar), three years before the death of Christopher Columbus, Nostradamus was a contemporary of Martin Luther and the Protestant Reformation. Now, centuries later, interest in the man and his prophecies is still keen.

His family was Jewish and had come from the vicinity of Avignon, France. His grandfather was Pierre de Nostredame, a grain dealer, who married a Gentile girl named Blanche. The seer's father, Jacques de Nostredame, escaped the family grain business and moved to St. Remy in 1493, where he married Regniere de St. Remy.

An edict concerning Jews was announced by King Louis XII on September 26, 1501. It gave all Jews three months to convert to Catholicism and be baptized into the Church or to leave Provence. The Nostredame family chose the Church and were listed in 1512 in local official records as part of the new Christian community. So Michel, who was Jewish by birth, was brought up in the Christian faith.

The young boy's extraordinary intellect was detected early. He was first taught by his grandfather, Jean de St. Remy, the rudiments of Latin, Greek, Hebrew, mathematics, and what he called the "celestial science," astrology. He was sent to Avignon to study, where he excelled and was known by his peers as "the little astrologer." The latter was due in part, perhaps, not only to his acumen in astrology, but also because he was shorter than average in height.

Astrology at that time included the understanding of the cycles of the sun and moon, the months and solemn feasts, and the interpretation of the mathematical positions of the planets in the heavens. Nostradamus believed that the earth revolved around the sun 100 years before Galileo was excommunicated from the Church for the same belief.

At age 19, Nostradamus entered the University of Montpelier to study medicine. In 1525, after rigorous study and examinations, he received his bachelor's degree and a license to practice medicine from the Bishop of Montpelier. During the next years he battled the "black plague" which ravaged southern France, showing great courage and compassion as a physician. Returning to the University of Montpelier, he earned his doctorate and the privilege to wear the distinctive black cap and cape and the gold ring of the physician. He taught at the University for one year, but his strong sense of independence and a certain wanderlust compelled him to move on. Although he was unorthodox in many of his methods of healing, his learning and ability were questioned neither by his contemporaries nor his interpreters and critics.

Known for his learning, Nostradamus was invited to stay at the home of Julius Cesar Scaliger, a Renaissance philosopher rated second only to Erasmus, the Dutch scholar. While there he married "a lady of high estate, very beautiful and admirable." They had two children and life was ideal; his practice was famous and profitable.

Then the plague struck again. As he fought the scourge, the renowned physician was unable to save his own family. His wife and two children died. More years of wanderings followed as he practiced his profession. He became known not only as a physician but also as a philosopher, astrologer, and prophet. At Aix in Provence he fought an outbreak of the plague, insisting on fresh air and unpolluted water. He prepared his own prescriptions from herbs, roses, and other plants. When the scourge subsided, he was given a lifetime pension by the city parliament.

Nostradamus then found a town to his liking, Salon-en-Provence, where he settled and spent the rest of his life. He married again in 1547 to a wealthy widow, Ann Ponsart Gemelle, and became the father of six more children. One of them, Cesar, was only 19 years old when his father died, but it is to him that we owe the account of the life of Nostradamus, which Cesar wrote in his *Histoire de Provence.*

Nostradamus lived most of his life favored by royal patronage, which included gifts, money, and honors. He was one of the few prophets whose talent and work supported him well. He lived the last 20 years of his life in Salon. His house still stands and is the hub of a thriving tourist trade. In 1566, ill with gout, arthritis, and dropsy, and as a doctor foreseeing his own death, Nostradamus summoned a notary to transcribe his will. He requested the last sacraments of the Church from Father Vidal, Superior of the Franciscan monastery at Salon.

Nostradamus asked to be buried in the church at the monastery. There, a marble slab was erected with the following epitaph: "Here rest the bones of the illustrious Michael Nostradamus, alone of all mortals judged worthy to record with his almost divine pen, under the influence of the stars, the future events of the entire world...."

Nostradamus was both reviled and revered during his lifetime. At Salon he was accused by some of being a tool of Satan, a Jew (although converted), and a Huguenot sympathizer. The latter accusation, in Catholic Provence, was a crime indeed. When his writings were published, although they were popular at court, some doctors and astrologers accused him of disgracing his professional status. He feared persecution by the Church, and was once summoned by the French Inquisition to face accusations by the clerics that he used "magic," a summons he successfully ignored.

The Prophecies of Nostradamus

The first published writings of Nostradamus were his yearly almanacs. The first of these, call *Almanac*, came out in 1550 when the seer was 47 years old and already established at Salon. The almanac contained predictions for the coming year and was an immediate success. For the rest of Nostradamus' life the yearly almanacs were popular and anticipated by the residents of Provence.

Five years later in 1555 the first part of *Prophecies* appeared. Nostradamus chose to write his predictions in what he called Centuries. A century was composed of 100 four-line verses called quatrains. His intentions were to write ten Centuries, totaling 1,000 quatrains which Nostradamus called a Milliade – a word for "a thousand verses." Part one of *Prophecies* consisted of Centuries I, II, III, and 53 quatrains of Century IV.

The prophecies are by no means in chronological order. The quatrains in part one extend from the time of Nostradamus to the "end of the world," as some interpret it. They are jumbled as to time periods. At the beginning of this section of the prophecies Nostradamus put an explanatory Preface addressed to his son Cesar. In it the father apprised his son of his beliefs concerning prophecy, his total faith in the sovereignty of God, and events he foresaw for the future.

Nostradamus had worked on *Prophecies* for some time without publishing them, realizing that when made public they would call down upon him criticisms, calumnies, and vicious backbiting. He was proved correct in this view. Much of the criticism came from other physicians and astrologers who were jealous of the success of the unorthodox doctor, and who used *Prophecies* as an opportunity to denounce Nostradamus.

Prophecies proved to be a success. On the strength of the verses, Nostradamus' fame spread over France and most of Europe. The prophet came under the good graces of Henri II and Catherine de Medici, king and queen of France. On more than one occasion he was summoned to their Court in Paris. In 1557 additional quatrains were added to part one of *Prophecies,* making seven Centuries in all. These were published in Lyons. For some reason known only to Nostradamus himself, Century VII in this edition and in all future editions remained incomplete. One wonders if Nostradamus withdrew quatrains which he did not wish to be made public.

It was to King Henri II that the completed volume of *Prophecies,* containing Centuries VIII through X, was dedicated. Dated June 27, 1558, the volume was not published until ten years later in 1568, two years after the death of Nostradamus. However, many of the new quatrains were circulated during his lifetime in manuscript form. The dedication to the completed *Prophecies* was in the form of a letter to Henri II and has come to be known as the *Epistle.* The letter contains in prose form a lengthy summary list of predictions for the near and far future. The paragraphs of the *Epistle* have been numbered and coded as have the quatrains of *Prophecies.* The quotations from the *Epistle* and *Prophecies* in this book will be identified by these numbers and codes.

In the *Epistle* Nostradamus expressed to Henri II and to all other intended readers his reaction to the false accusations of his critics. He wrote, "There are some who would attribute to me that which is not mine at all. The eternal God alone, who is the thorough searcher of human hearts, pious, just and merciful, is the true judge, and it is to Him I pray to defend me from the calumny of evil men" (E 8). A few lines later in the *Epistle* Nostradamus declared his faith in "our Savior and Redeemer, Jesus Christ, born of the unique Virgin" (E 10).

Of Jewish birth and Christian faith, he was always firm in his belief that his gift of prophecy came from God. He was also firm in his belief that his work would endure. He wrote, "...As time elapses after my death, my writings will have more weight than during my lifetime. Should I, however, have made any errors in my calculations of dates, or prove unable to please everybody, I beg that your more than Imperial Majesty will forgive me. I protest before God and His Saints that I do not propose to insert any writings in this present Epistle that will be contrary to the true Catholic faith, whilst consulting the astronomical calculations to the best of my ability" (E 9).

Nostradamus was always quite open about the sources of his prophecies. He used the Scriptures, he used astrology to date events, and he relied on his own intuition. Alone in his study at night, he was given visions. He was emphatic in asserting that whatever the means, the messages came from God. He wrote in the *Epistle,* "I present these predictions almost with confusion, especially as to when they will take place. ...The chronology of time....was determined by astronomy and other sources, including the Holy Scriptures, and thus could not err....I have calculated the present prophecies...all by astronomical doctrine modified by my natural instinct" (E 39, 41).

In another place in the *Epistle* he wrote, "I readily admit that all proceeds from God and render to Him thanks, honor and immortal praise. I have mixed therewith no divination coming from fate. All from God and nature, and for the most part integrated with celestial movements" (E 9).

As an astrologer-astronomer Nostradamus was aware that the sun, moon, and planets move in precise, predictable patterns through the heavens. He knew that their positions are identified by their orbits through the twelve signs of the zodiac, in a precise order, at a precise speed. Clocks and calendars may err, but the celestial bodies are always on time. So by this method Nostradamus often timed future events.

Two examples of his dating by means of astrology are taken from Century IV: "the year that Saturn will be conjoined in Aquarius with the Sun" (IV.86) and "in the year that Mars, Venus, and the Sun are in conjunction in summer" (IV.84). The first conjunction quoted happens about every 29 years. The second quoted occurs more often. In both instances Nostradamus gives a specific time to look for, but he does not give the year. This is one of the factors that make some of his prophecies obscure.

It is of interest to note that Nostradamus mentions the planet Neptune, although Neptune was not discovered until 1846. The quatrain reads in part, "...Venus hidden under the whiteness of Neptune..." (IV.33). He also mentions Vulcan (IV.29), a planet that some astrologers believe is waiting to be discovered.

There were times, however, when Nostradamus did not revert to the use of the planets' placements to determine dates. One instance is a quatrain which is significant for our own time. "In the year 1999, seventh month, from the sky will come a great King of Terror..." (X.72). This is one to ponder.

Several facts are clear about the prophecies of Nostradamus. An important one is that Nostradamus knew more than he passed on to posterity. Also, most of the prophecies which he did pass on are not easy to interpret.

Nostradamus deliberately obscured many of his predictions. He had his reasons. He was at the mercy of certain officials of the Church and at the mercy of the King. He was under scrutiny of the populace, especially the intellectuals, who since the beginning of the Renaissance were no longer under intellectual subjection. He did not want to offend the persons whose patronage he enjoyed. He did not want to be caught with predictions that did not come to pass. Therefore, he often took the easy (and wise) way out and clouded what he wrote.

His own words tell us that this is so. To his son Cesar he wrote: "I decided to write by dark and cryptic sentences in a manner that would not upset their fragile sentiments" (Preface 6). Nostradamus was referring to "the great ones of kingdoms, sects, religions and faiths which would find so little in accord with what their fancy would like to hear" (P 5). He added, "All had to be written under a cloudy figure, especially things prophetic" (P 6). Nostradamus, quoting Scripture, wrote in the Preface to Cesar that he preferred to heed the admonition not to "cast your pearls before swine, lest they trample them under their feet and turn and rend you" (P 5).

Then why did he write the prophecies at all? "... Because all these things proceeded from the divine power of the great eternal God, from who all goodness flows" (P 10). In the Preface Nostradamus also expressed his opinion of himself as a prophet. "Furthermore, my son, though I have mentioned the name prophet, I do not wish to assume for myself a title so sublime for the present" (P 11). Again Nostradamus said concerning his prophecies, "I have sought to polish them a bit obscurely" (P 19).

Nostradamus wrote in a motley of languages – French, Provencal, Italian, Greek, and Latin – which increases the difficulties in interpreting the quatrains. Added to the inherent ambiguities of the verses, some translators and interpreters either knowingly or unwittingly have distorted the quatrains, making them say what they really did not say. After the prophet's death, verses on several occasions appeared which were falsely claimed to have been written by Nostradamus. All these things make interpreting his words difficult.

Nostradamus had ingenious methods of obscuring his prophecies. He used anagrams, which is changing the letters or inserted extra letters in words. He used words that were no longer in use at the time. In short, Nostradamus did what he deliberately set out to do, which was to confuse the reader.

In spite of the ambiguities of his work, Nostradamus wrote of a future time when the prophecies would be clearer than in his own day. After writing of far future famine, pestilence, and war, he then stated, "For the mercy of the Lord, my son, shall not be extended at all for a long time, not until most of my prophecies will have been accomplished, and will by accomplishment have become resolved... For although they are written under a cloud, the meanings will be understood. When the time comes for the removal of ignorance, the event will be cleared up still more" (P 32,33).

Fulfilled Prophecies

Nostradamus was not infallible. It was common knowledge that he made some erroneous predictions. Like the American seeress, Jeane Dixon, he at times did not correctly understand the visions he saw. But the number of his prophecies which have already been fulfilled is truly amazing. His predictions, which already can be seen to have been correct, spanned four centuries. He foresaw Napoleon Bonaparte and Adolph Hitler, calling them the first and second antichrists. He saw the downfall of the Shah of Iran and the ascendance of the Ayatollah. Following are some of his fulfilled prophecies.

• Over one hundred years before it happened, Nostradamus predicted the great fire of London which in 1666 very nearly wiped out the old City, which had begun as a trading post of the Roman Empire in 43 A.D. On the night of the fire people rushed from their burning wooden homes into St. Paul's Cathedral, made of stone, hoping to find safety. But the great old church was also destroyed along with the people inside it.

> "The blood of the just will make a mistake at London.
> Burned through lightning of twenty threes and six:
> The ancient lady will fall from her high place,
> Several of the same sect will be destroyed" (II.51).

The popular interpretation of this quatrain is that the words "twenty threes and six" are the last two digits of 1666, the "ancient lady" is the cathedral, and "several of the same sect" indicates the other churches of the City which were also destroyed.

• The prophet foresaw the French Revolution which began in 1789, calling it "the vulgar event," probably using vulgar in the best sense of the word meaning of the people. He predicted the arrest in 1791 of King Louis XVI and Marie Antoinette, naming the town where they were seized, Varennes, and even describing the color of the clothes they wore, the king in gray and his wife in white.

House of Napoleon's Mother

This house in the heart of Rome is the place Napoleon Bonaparte secured to be the home of his Corsican mother. The house, stately and comfortable, still stands as a tangible reminder of the man Nostradamus called the "first antichrist."

Powerful dictators have been fascinated by Rome. The man whom Nostradamus called the "second antichrist" – Adolph Hitler – expected his Third Reich to be the third Roman Empire. In Paris, Napoleon's French capital, there is a tall statue in the beautiful center of the city of lights. It is a statue of Napoleon, commissioned by himself, of the dictator dressed in a Roman toga and wearing the Roman laurel wreath of victory on his head.

The quatrain reads,

"By night will come through the forest of Reines,
Two by a roundabout route, the queen a white stone
The king monkish in gray in Varennes:
The chosen Capet causes storm, fire, blood, slice"
(IX.20).

Capet was the name of the dynasty of French kings. As for the fate of Louis XVI and Marie Antoinette by the guillotine, an apt description is "bloody slicing."

• Nostradamus named Napoleon the first antichrist. He also called him a "thunderbolt."

"Of the name which no Gallic King ever had
Never was there so fearful a thunderbolt,
Causing Italy, Spain, and the English to tremble,
Very attentive to foreign women" (IV.54).

Napoleon was the first French crowned monarch to be called by that name. He was married to Josephine, a Creole from the West Indies, and to Marie Louise of Austria.

• Nostradamus saw the downfall of Napoleon and described the places of his two banishments.

"The great Empire will soon be exchanged
For a small place which very soon will come to grow:
A very tiny place in a flat land
Where in its midst he will come to put down his
scepter" (I.32).

Thus the prophet pictured the dictator's end as the exchange of a great Empire for a small place (the island of Elba) and then a smaller place (the island of Helena).

• Nostradamus predicted the gradual failure of the League of Nations.

"The tiresome sermons from the Lake of Geneva
From days will decline to weeks,
Then months, then years, then all will fail,
The Magistrates will damn their useless laws" (I.47).

After years of fruitless argument and failure, the League of Nations formally disbanded in August 1947.

• Adolph Hitler was designated as the second antichrist by Nostradamus. He was called a captain of Great Germany.

"A captain of Great Germany
Will come to deliver through false hope...
So that his revolt will cause a great flow of blood"
(IX.90).

Nostradamus may have described the swastika, the symbol of the Nazis, as a crooked cross in the following quatrain. Mars was the Roman god of war.

"The great leader of the party of Mars
Will subjugate the confines of the Danube:
Pursuing with sword and a crooked cross,
Captives, gold, jewels to more than one hundred
thousand rubies" (VI.49).

In the Epistle, Nostradamus wrote of the actions of this second antichrist. "It will be at this time and in these countries that the infernal power will set the power of its adversaries against the Church of Jesus Christ. This will constitute the second antichrist who will persecute that Church and its true Vicar, by means of the power of three temporal kings who in their ignorance will be seduced by tongues which, in the hands of madmen, will cut more than any sword" (E 45).

- One of the quatrains from Nostradamus which convinced Hitler to hire an astrologer predicted that a great man of the people would come from Austria, the birthplace of Hitler the commoner. This leader would "defend" Poland and Hungary.

"Near the Rhine from the Noric mountains (Austria)
Will be born a great one of the people...
Who will defend Saurome (Poland) and the
Pannoniques (Hungarians),
No one will know what will have become of him"
(III.58).

The last line of the quatrain, which Hitler apparently ignored, seems to describe the mystery still surrounding Hitler's last hours in the bunker at Berlin.

The chief astrologer whom Hitler engaged was Hans Ernst Krafft, who for a time could tell Hitler what he wanted to hear. When his scholarship prevented Krafft from continuing to satisfy the Fuhrer's demands, the astrologer was arrested. Krafft died on the way to a concentration camp.

• Nostradamus predicted the establishment of a new land, which no doubt means the State of Israel.

"A new law will occupy a new land
Toward Syria, Judea, and Palestine..." (III.97).

• This group of already fulfilled prophecies of Nostradamus will close with the following two concerning the decline of communism, which he predicted even before its rise. This quatrain locates the beginning of its fall.

"The law of Utopia will be seen to decline,
After another much more seductive:
The Dnieper River first will give way,
Through gifts and a tongue more attractive" (III.95).

The Dnieper River flows through the Ukraine and Lithuania. The next quatrain speaks of our time.

"In the places and times of flesh giving way to fish,
The communal law will face opposition:
It will hold strongly the old ones, then removed,
Communism put far behind" (IV.32)

This seems to indicate that the old guard is the last to go. Does the first line mean that people are eating less meat and more fish? Nostradamus indeed looked far ahead.

Prophecies for the Future

The prophecies which Nostradamus made about the future, during and beyond our day, are having a resurgence in popularity. Like other predictors of the Christian age, he made forecasts that closely parallel those in the Bible. Since the Bible pre-dates the works of these prophets, one may raise the question of whether or not their predictions were taken from the Scriptures. Still the similarities are interesting, especially in regard to the seers' sequencing of events compared to the sequencing found in the Bible. In general, most of the forecasters as well as the Bible have predicted for our future a great and terrible war and then a time of enduring peace.

• One of Nostradamus' prophecies which parallels the Bible concerns "...the procreation of the new Babylon....which will last for only seventy-three years and seven months" (E 25). Iraq (the new Babylon) was established in 1921, when its leaders gave the country of ancient Babylonia its new name Iraq and elected the first monarch. Seventy-three years, the length of life Nostradamus predicted for Iraq, added to 1921 is 1994.

The Bible says concerning the reborn Babylon, *"...Babylon the great is fallen....Alas, alas, that great city...in one hour she is made desolate....Thus with violence the great city Babylon shall be thrown down, and shall not be found anymore"* (Revelation 18:2,19,21).

Nostradamus described the burning of a great new city.

"At 45 degrees the sky will burn,
Fire approaches the great new city,
Instantly a great scattered flame will leap up..."
(VI.97).

The Temple Site

Standing on the old stones of the Temple area, where Jesus had predicted its destruction, one can see the Mount of Olives rising above the horizon toward the east. During the last week of Jesus' earthly life, He traveled each day between the mount and the Temple.

Each morning He entered the Temple to teach the people who gathered there. Each evening He returned to the Mount of Olives to spend the night on the ground under the olive trees.

He saw the Mount of Olives the first time during the Passover festival when He was a boy of twelve. It was His first glimpse of the 100,000 or so Jewish pilgrims who the historian Josephus said encamped along the ridge of the mount when they came to Jerusalem for a holy festival. On the mount, as Messiah, he made many prophecies about events still in our future.

The old city of Babylon is currently being rebuilt by Saddam Hussein near 45 degrees east longitude.

• Nostradamus predicted that in his distant future people would experience wars and natural disasters which had not as yet been seen. "...They will be overwhelmed and slaughtered...There will be signs and great earthquakes...Oh, what a clamitous affliction will pregnant women bear...Great desolation will come" (E 22,25,35,34).

Jesus in His sermon on the Mount of Olives, commonly called the Olivet Discourse, spoke of the same occurrences. *"You will hear of wars and rumors of war....There will be famines, pestilences, and earthquakes...Woe to those who are pregnant....There will be a great tribulation...signs and wonders"* (Matthew 24:6,7,19,21,24).

• Nostradamus named the month of October as the time when believers in Christ will be taken from the earth in what is known in Christian theology as the Rapture of the Church. "...The coming of the Holy Ghost...will make a transmigration...It will be in the month of October that the great translation will take place..." (E 23,24).

The apostle Paul also wrote about the translation of the church. *"For the Lord himself will descend from heaven with a shout...and the dead in Christ will rise first. Then we who are alive...shall be caught up together with them in the clouds to meet the Lord in the air..."* (1 Thessalonians 4:16,17).

• Nostradamus predicted a revival of the old Roman Empire. "...The Roman people will begin to re-establish themselves...recovering some of their ancient glory. But this will not be without great division and continual changes. Thereafter...it will be not far short of the strength of ancient Rome" (E 43).

The prophet Daniel in the sixth century B.C. prophesied the same strength, the same divisions. *"The kingdom will be partly strong and partly fragile...They will not adhere to one another...And in the days of these kings the God of heaven will set up a kingdom which shall never be destroyed"* (Daniel 2:42-44). Daniel wrote these words concerning the revival of the old Roman Empire, which may have its beginning in the formation of the European Economic Community and the United States of Europe.

• Nostradamus made a number of predictions about the third Antichrist, who closely resembles the Antichrist of Scripture. "...Antichrist will be the infernal prince....By means of Satan, Prince Infernal, so many evils will be committed that nearly all the world will find itself undone and desolated....Wars will be grievous....Strange birds will cry in the air, 'Today, today'..." (E 55).

While banished to the Isle of Patmos, the apostle John was shown a vision of the Antichrist to come. *"...I saw a beast (Antichrist) rise out of the sea....And Satan gave him his power, his throne, and great authority....Power was given to kill with sword, with hunger, with death...And all the birds were filled with their flesh"* (Revelation 13:1,2;6:8;19:21).

• Nostradamus predicted the chaining of Satan and then an era of peace. "Hearing the affliction of His people, God the Creator will command Satan to be cast into the bottomless pit, and bound there. Then a universal peace will begin...And Satan will remain bound for a thousand years, and then unbound" (E 56).

In his Patmos vision the apostle John saw a similar development. *"An angel laid hold of Satan and bound him for a thousand years....Afterward he must be released for a little while....Blessed is he...who shall reign with Christ a thousand years"* (Revelation 20:2,3,6).

The End of the Papacy

Nostradamus, along with two other notable prophets, made some interesting predictions about the popes who were to be the last to hold the papal office. As the papacy was to run its final course, the three foreseers provided details concerning the last seven vicars of Rome. Incidentally or not, the three prophets – Nostradamus of France, St. Malachy of Ireland, and American Jeane Dixon – are all considered to be devout members of the Roman Catholic Church.

The first of the last seven popes, according to the reckoning of the predictors, was Pius XII (1939–1958). Following him have been John XXIII (1958–1963), Paul VI (1963–1978), John Paul I (1978), and John Paul II (1978–). The prophets have said that two more popes are to come.

Besides predicting the end of the papacy, St. Malachy who lived in the twelfth century A.D. described 112 popes who would succeed Innocent II, the pope when Malachy prophesied. Tradition has it that the Irish prophet gave the list of descriptions to Innocent II, who stashed the manuscript in the Vatican archives, where it stayed for 400 years and was then published in 1597. The descriptions of the coming popes were written in Latin

The Vatican Gardens

The gardens near St. Peter's Church in Vatican City bloom profusely with Mediterannean flowers. The white walks and splendid statuary amid the vegetation province a place of serenity.

Since the eighth century in the days of Pepin the Short, who was Charlemagne's father, the one hundred and eight acres of land within the city of Rome have been the home of the Roman Catholic popes. Pepin, in return for certain favors like approval of his marriage, gave Pope Stephen II military aid against a Lombard king. After a victory on the battlefield, Pepin gave the pope the land that is now Vatican City. The gardens above are one of its most beautiful areas.

More than one prophet has predicted that there will be only two more popes after the present one to enjoy the idyllic scene.

and were confined to mere phrases.

The pontiffs mentioned above were characterized by Malachy as follows: Pius XII as the "angel shepherd," John XXIII as "pastor and sailor," Paul VI as "flower of flowers," John Paul I as "of the middle of the moon," and John Paul II as "of the labor of the sun." The two popes who are to follow John Paul II were give the inscriptions by Malachy as "the glory of the olive" and "Peter the Roman." Then, according to Malachy, will end the papacy.

St. Malachy's descriptions are interesting. John Paul I, "of the middle of the moon," who lived as pope only 33 days, died midway between two full moons. According to three quatrains of Nostradamus, John Paul I was murdered by poison.

Of the two future popes, "the glory of the olive" may be a peace maker, extending the olive branch. Malachy predicted that such a peace would be short. "Peter the Roman" Malachy foresaw as living in a time of tribulation when the Church would be persecuted. After this, he prophesied, Rome – the City of Seven Hills – will be destroyed.

Like Nostradamus and Malachy, Jeane Dixon foresaw bodily harm to one pope and the assassination of another. Like them she also saw a coming dreadful persecution of the Christian church. But by far her most astounding predictions surround the person who will be responsible for the persecution – the "third Antichrist" seen by Nostradamus and the Antichrist of Scripture. Jeane Dixon, moreover, has specifically named the hour of the birth of this man to have been February 5, 1962, shortly after seven a.m. Washington, D.C., time.

Jeane Dixon

Jeane Dixon is the well-known seeress living in the nation's capital, who from the 1930's through the 1970's advised friends, persons she just met, and government officials on the basis of what she saw as a psychic. Her crystal ball at Washington parties was a source of information for those who asked. President Franklin Roosevelt consulted her. Her predictions of events which later occurred, including the assassination of President John F. Kennedy, were well documented.

When Dixon sees events before they happen, she makes no attempt to explain the how or why of her visions. She does not analyze; she only reports what she sees. Concerning her gift, she has observed, "The Bible says, 'Ask and ye shall receive.' I ask God to show me anything which I should be able to tell others for the enlightenment and betterment of mankind. I think that He is the best judge of what I should know."

Jeane Dixon was taught astrology when she was in her teens by a Jesuit priest, but her predictions about the future have not come through astrology. She considers astrology too time-consuming. She has received her important forecasts through visions, which have appeared to her when she did not expect them. She receives the visions unsought, but she must interpret them herself. When events do not come to pass as she has predicted them, she still stands by the visions. They are always correct, she says. But at times she admittedly misreads their meaning. Sometimes she corrects her first mistaken interpretation. An example of what she now calls a misinterpretation of a vision is the one concerning

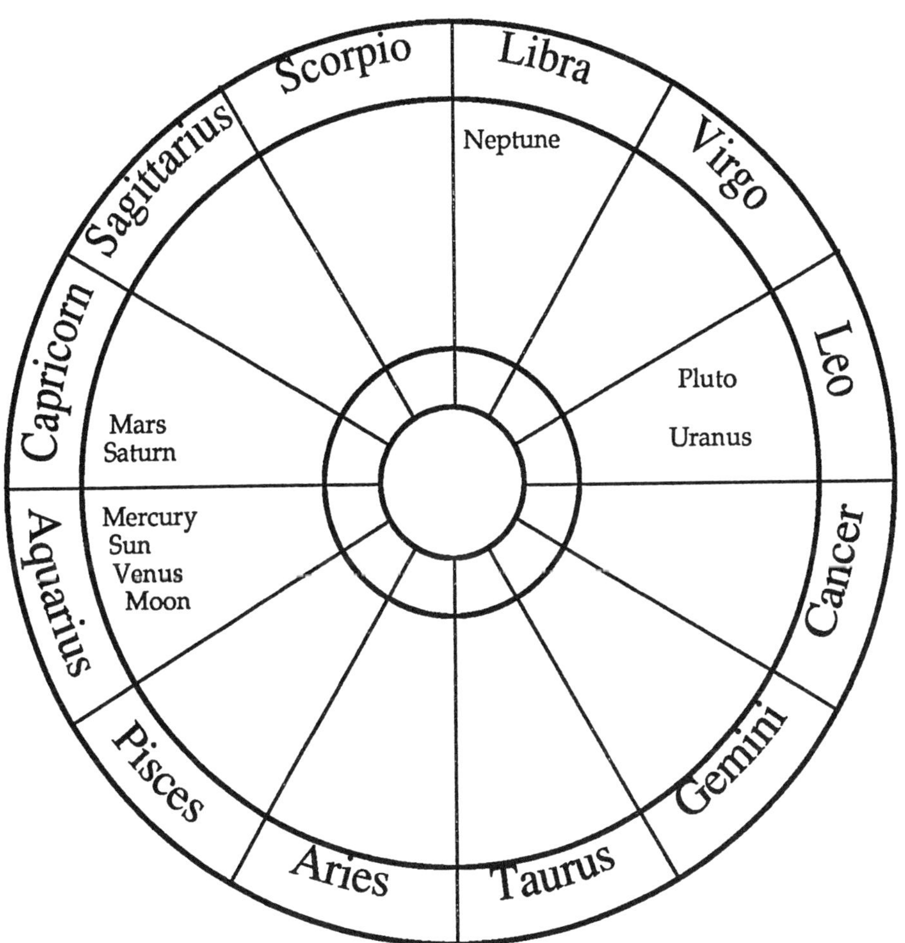

Birth Chart of Child
February 5, 1962, 7:15 EST
Ascendant is 13 Degrees Aquarius

the birth of the child who was born on February 5, 1962. Her first interpretation, which she later considered to be incorrect, was recorded in a book about the seeress, *A Gift of Prophecy,* written by Ruth Montgomery and published in 1965. Later, in her own book, *My Life and Prophecies,* Mrs. Dixon changed her interpretation of the meaning of the vision.

Long before Jeane Dixon received the vision of the child, astrologers had studied that date in Feburary because of its astrological significance. Its striking importance came from the fact that on that day in the heavens there was a preponderance of planets and luminaries in the zodiacal sign Aquarius. Clustered together in that one sign were the Sun, Moon, Mercury, Venus, Mars, Jupiter, and Saturn. In astrology when planets are in conjunction they strengthen each other. Two or three planets in conjunction strongly influence a birth chart. Seven together are indeed remarkable.

Astrologers have marveled at the abundance of Aquarian characteristics in the personalities of the children born on that day. These children, who are now adults, are humanitarian, friendly, outgoing, independent, unpredictable, with good business sense, and a likelihood for success. They have striking intellects and in all probability are very attractive.

The early hour of the birth of the child in Jeane Dixon's vision, soon after seven a.m., gives that particular child an Aquarian ascendant or rising sign, increasing even more the Aquarian tendencies of his nature. From the beginning Jeane Dixon was certain that the child was to have great revolutionary impact on the whole world. What changed in her interpretations was the kind of impact. At first she thought that his influence would be for good. This is the view she later changed.

The vision revealed that the child was born somewhere in the Middle East of humble peasant parents, but the decendant of a royal Egyptian line. Dixon saw wisdom and knowledge showing forth from the child's eyes and considered him to be the answer to the prayers of a troubled world. Later, however, in her own book she interpreted the baby to be the Antichrist, a person who would have sweeping power over the earth and who would be inherently evil. The latter interpretation came after much meditation, prayer, and study of the Scriptures under the tutelage of Cardinal Newman.

Dixon now believes the child is the Antichrist of the Bible. In a subsequent vision she saw him as a boy in his twelfth year becoming aware of his diabolical mission. This mimics Jesus the true Christ as a boy of twelve talking with the doctors in the temple, aware of who His Father was.

The person in Dixon's visions, according to what she sees, is now being groomed for his emergence on the public scene. When that happens, he will promise to a believing and enraptured world that he will bring peace, prosperity, and spiritual satisfaction. But in the end all he can deliver will be disaster.

The predictions Jeane Dixon made over 22 years ago parallel the biblical prophecies of a coming world conflagration. She missed the timing, however, on one of her more startling prophecies. She saw the beginning of World War III in a conflict between China and the United States to occur in the 1980's. As events turned out, the confrontation was revolution within China itself. The lowering of moral standards, which Dixon predicted would result in the holocaustal sufferings of our own and other nations, indeed had roots in the 'eighties. The seeds for the sufferings she has predicted have been planted – greed, extravagance, blatant dishonesty, and moral disintegration in government, business, and society. Dixon also believes, however, that the time will come, as the Bible also predicts, when "we will all be united in the Brotherhood of Christ under the Fatherhood of God."

Signs of the Times

The Bible never sets specific dates. Instead, it tells us to read the signs of the times. Jesus spoke about date-setting and watching for the signs of the times on at least three occasions.

One was when He stood with the disciples and other believers, 40 days after His resurrection, on the Mount of Olives. It was just before He ascended to the Father in heaven. The disciples asked, "*...'Lord, will You at this time restore the kingdom to Israel?' And He said to them, 'It is not for you to know times or seasons which the Father has put in His own authority'*" (Acts 1:6,7).

After Jesus ascended into heaven, two angels appeared and prophesied that Jesus would return to the earth. "*...While they watched, He was taken up, and a cloud received Him out of their sight. And while they looked steadfastly toward heaven as He went up, behold, two men stood by them in white apparel, who also said, 'Men of Galilee, why do you stand gazing up into heaven? This same Jesus, who was taken up from you into heaven, will so come in like manner as you saw Him go into heaven'*" (Acts 1:9-11).

Jesus had already instructed them to read the signs of the times. He had said to the Pharisees and Sadducees in the hearing of the disciples, "...*When it is evening you say, 'It will be fair weather, for the sky is red'; and in the morning, 'It will be foul weather today, for the sky is red and threatening.' Hypocrites! You know how to discern the face of the sky, but you cannot discern the signs of the times*" (Matthew 16:2,3).

Jesus had repeated to the disciples during the last week of His life on earth, again on the Mount of Olives, that they were to read the signs of the times. Jesus spoke a parable to them and called the budding fig tree a sign of the times. "*They asked him, saying, '...What sign will there be when these things are about to take place?....And he spoke to them a parable: 'Look at the fig tree, and all the trees. When they are already budding, you see and know for yourselves that summer is near. So you, likewise, when you see these things happening, know that the kingdom of God is near*" (Luke 21:7,29-31).

The fig tree in the Bible always represents Israel. The other trees are the other nations. Jesus was saying to the disciples, "When Israel begins to bud, know that my return is near."

Allegory of the Trees

There is an allegory about the trees as nations in the book of Judges. It was written when a man wrongfully usurped power over a nation.

> *"The trees once went forth to anoint a king over them.*
> *And they said to the olive tree, 'Reign over us!'*

But the olive tree said to them,
'Should I cease my giving oil,
Which honors God and men,
And go to hold sway over the trees?'

"Then the trees said to the fig tree,
'You come and reign over us!'
But the fig tree said to them,
'Should I cease my sweetness and my good fruit
And go to hold sway over trees?'

"Then the trees said to the vine,
'You come and reign over us!'
But the vine said to them,
'Should I cease my new wine,
Which cheers both God and men,
And go to hold sway over trees?'

"Then all the trees said to the bramble,
'You come and reign over us!'
And the bramble said to the trees,
'If in truth you anoint me as king over you,
Then come and take shelter in my shade;
But if not, let fire come out of the bramble
And devour the cedars of Lebanon!'"

(Judges 9:8-15)

In this allegory of the trees, the larger meaning centers on the time when the nations will give up their sovereignty and give the Antichrist power over them. The result will be that fire will come out of the bramble (the Antichrist) to devour the cedars (the nations).

The Fig Tree

The fig tree in the Holy Land is a prized commodity. It gives shade from the sun, and its fruit is a sweet, juicy repast on a summer day in a hot land.

The fig tree in the Bible represents the nation Israel. In the figurative language of Scripture, the barren fig tree means the nation is barren. When belligerent countries harm the fig tree, they harm Israel. When the fig tree is beginning to bud, something is beginning to happen in Israel. In Bible prophecy the fig tree is always Israel.

Jesus used the figure of the fig tree when He spoke of what was to come. When He passed the fig tree that produced no fruit, he cursed it. His disciples were amazed the next day to find it dead.

When Jesus spoke of future events, He used the fig tree as one of the signs of the times. He said to watch the fig tree. When it begins to bud, He said, know that summer is nigh.

However, there is another meaning for today when many nations are throwing off the brambles of unjust tyranny. This is one of the signs of the times which Jesus indicated when He said, *"Look at the fig tree, and all the trees."*

The budding of the fig tree is the establishment of the state of Israel, the blossoming of the land, and the return of many Jews to the land of Israel. Before May 14, 1948, when the state of Israel was formed by the United Nations, the Bible prophecies concerning Israel and the return of Christ could not have been fulfilled. But now that Israel exists as a nation, those predictions can come to pass. The same metaphor is used in the book of Hosea, as the Lord speaks, *"I found Israel...as the firstfruits on the fig tree in its first season..."* (Hosea 9:10).

The current immigration of Jews to Israel is another example of the predicted signs of the times. For over 2500 years ago the prophet Ezekiel spoke the words of the Lord, *"I will take you from among the nations, gather you out of all countries, and bring you into your own land"* (Ezekiel 36:24).

Almost a century before Ezekiel, the prophet Jeremiah prophesied the return of the Jews to Israel from the north country. *"'...The days are coming,' says the Lord, 'that they shall no longer say, 'As the Lord lives who brought up the children of Israel from the land of Egypt,' but, 'As the Lord lives who brought up and led the descendants of the house of Israel from the north country...'"* (Jeremiah 23:7,8). Russia is north of Israel, and already over a quarter of a million Russian Jews have immigrated to Israel.

A century before Jeremiah, the prophet Isaiah wrote, *"Who are these who fly like a cloud, and like doves to their roosts...to bring your sons from afar...?"* (Isaiah 60:8,9). Long

Ruins at Capernaum

Capernaum, the town which Jesus chose as headquarters for His Galilean ministry, was on the northwest shore of the Sea of Galilee. Here He performed many miracles. Here He called Matthew the tax-collector to be His disciple, luring him from the Roman customs office. Capernaum was a town of considerable size to have had this government facility.

The synagogue in Capernaum in Jesus' day was built by the Roman centurion whose servant Jesus healed. The ruins in the photograph are from a later synagogue of the third or fourth century. The symbols carved in the ruins combine Graeco-Roman architecture with Jewish symbols such as palm leaves, stars, and grapes.

Jesus predicted the destruction of Capernaum because of its rejection of Him, adding that it would never be rebuilt. Today it is in ruins. In 1905 a German archaeological expedition uncovered the ruins of this synagogue. Under it was the floor of an older synagogue, the one in which Jesus taught.

before the airplane the Lord said, *"...I bore you on eagles' wings and brought you to Myself"* (Exodus 19:4). These prophecies were fulfilled in Operation Magic Carpet which brought the Yemen Jews to Israel, and in Operation Solomon which flew the Ethiopian Jews back to the land. Both these groups were from the south of Israel. *"I will say...to the south, 'Do not keep them back!' Bring My sons from afar, and My daughters from the ends of the earth"* (Isaiah 43:6).

Sure Prophecy of the Bible

The fulfillment of Bible prophecy is sure. The timing of the Bible prophecy is sure. There have been people who, in some manner, have broken through the time barrier and made predictions which proved to be true. But the only sure prophecies – absolutely without error – are to be found in the Bible. The apostle Peter declared the prophecy in Scripture to be true. *"We have a more sure word of prophecy..."* (2 Peter 1:19).

One past fulfilled Bible prophecy concerns the town of Capernaum on the shore of the Sea of Gallilee. Jesus prophecied that the town would be destroyed because of the people's unbelief. *"He began to upbraid the cities in which most of His mighty works had been done, because they did not repent. '...You, Capernaum, who are exalted to heaven, will be brought down...for if the mighty works which were done in you had been done in Sodom, it would have remained until this day'"* (Matthew 11:20,23). A town of considerable size in Jesus' day, Capernaum has disappeared, with only the archaeologists' digs and the foosteps of tourists to disturb the serenity of the Galilean scene. True to prophecy,

The Wailing Wall

All that remains of Herod's magnificent third temple is a remnant of the outer enclosure, called the Wailing Wall.

Until 1967 the area was part of the Arab kingdom of Jordan. Since the Six Days War, Jews have returned daily to lament their lost former glory. They and others put prayers written on small pieces of paper and rolled into tiny cylinders into the cracks of the wall.

When the Roman general Titus came in A.D. 70 with his legions to quell the hotbed of rebellion in Jerusalem, he intended to spare the Temple. Titus was firm in his desire not to destroy the resplendent gold and marble edifice which had taken over 46 years to build. The frenzied resistance of the Jews, however, led to its burning and destruction. This assured the fulfillment of the prophecy of Jesus, *"...I say to you, not one stone shall be left here upon another, that shall not be thrown down"* (Matthew 24:2).

Capernaum has never been rebuilt.

Another past fulfilled prophecy concerns the magnificent temple of Jesus' day, located in Jerusalem. Forty years in the building, it was called Herod's Temple because he refurbished and adorned it for the Jews. When His disciples remarked on the grandeur of the structure, Jesus said, *"As for these things which you see, the days will come in which not one stone shall be left upon another that shall not be thrown down"* (Luke 21:6). The temple was destroyed in 70 A.D. by the Roman army. True to Jesus' words, not one stone was left upon another. All that remains today is the western retaining wall of the temple complex, not a part of the temple itself, which is known as the Wailing Wall.

In the Old Testament it was predicted that the Northern Kingdom of Israel would be overrun by the Assyrians and the people would be deported, never to return. That was the way it happened. It was predicted that the Southern Kingdom of Judah would be invaded by the Babylonians, the people would be deported, and after 70 years they would be permitted to return. That is the way it turned out.

Since all Bible prophecy has been fulfilled like clockwork so far, it is reasonable to believe that Bible prophecy which remains for the future will likewise be fulfilled on schedule. The preliminaries for its fulfillment are rapidly being set in place.

Why Study Bible Prophecy?

What reason does a person have for studying Bible prophecy? There are three good reasons. First and foremost we become privy to the plans and purposes of God. From the beginning to the end of history God has let people in on his plans. This is emphatically stated in the Bible. God in the prophecy of Isaiah declared,

> *"...I am God, and there is no other;*
> *I am God, and there is none like Me,*
> *Declaring the end from the beginning,*
> *And from ancient times things that are*
> *not yet done...*
> *Indeed I have spoken it;*
> *I will also bring it to pass.*
> *I have purposed it;*
> *I will also do it"* (Isaiah 46:9-11).

When a dear friend projects plans for the future and shares them, we have an intimate relationship with that friend. A great scholar of Bible prophecy, Dr. C. I. Scofield, said about the prophecies in the Scriptures, "These are the great truths which God gives us who are His children. He unfolds for us the magnificent future, and shows us our relation to that future." The revelations intrusted to us fill us with holy and happy expectations.

Prophecy and Action

The second reason for studying Bible prophecy is that its disclosure inevitably affects our character and conduct. The apostle Peter in a letter to the early Christians wrote an amazing prophecy about what eventually will happen to the planet earth. *"The Lord...is longsuffering toward us, not willing that any should perish but that all should come to repentance. But the day of the Lord will come as a thief in the night, in which the heavens will pass away with a great noise, and the elements will melt with fervent heat; both the earth and the works that are in it will be burned up"* (2 Peter 3:9,10).

Then Peter told what effect the prophecy should have on those who hear it. *"Therefore, since all these things will be dissolved, what manner of persons ought you to be in holy conduct and godliness?"* (2 Peter 3:11). Peter then adds that marvelous promise of God, *"Nevertheless we, according to His promise, look for new heavens and a new earth in which righteousness dwells"* (2 Peter 3:13). How natural it is to slough off unworthy thoughts and acts when we know the truth and consequences of all things.

Blessings On Those Who Heed

The third reason for the study of Bible prophecy is that it brings a distinct promise of blessing to those who inquire into it. The last book of the Bible contains this assurance of blessing. The Revelation of Jesus Christ reads, *"Blessed is he (she) who reads and those who hear the words of this prophecy, and keep those things which are written in it..."* (Revelation 1:3).

The promises of blessing are amplified in both figurative and concrete language.

"To him (her) who overcomes I will give to eat from the tree of life, which is in the midst of the Paradise of God....

"I will give some of the hidden manna to eat....

"I will give him a white stone, and on the stone a new name written....

"I will give power over the nations...and I will give him the

morning star....

"He shall be clothed in white garments....

"I will come in to him and dine with him, and he with me....

"I will grant to sit with Me on My throne...."

(Revelation 2 and 3).

Like the prophets and seers of times past, one can understand a great deal of the past and future. We shall see that Bible prophecy is correlated with the astrological ages, those long periods of time which are written in the stars. The prophecy in Scripture also corresponds with the succession of the anthropological ages, the relics of which the scientists have uncovered in the ground. Astrology, the oldest science, and archaelogy, one of the newest, both attest to a synthesis of truth wherever it is found. The Bible affirms them both.

So now let us go to the beginning, when the stars were born.

Chapter 2

The Astrogical Ages

We are now living in the Age of Pisces and will soon enter the Age of Aquarius. These ages are two of a series of seven astrological ages which have succeeded each other since the creation of the human species called *homo sapiens*. We have come a long way so far, about 12,000 years.

The Ages in the Stars

The astrological ages get their names from the twelve constellations which can be seen beyond the planets of the solar system. The astrological ages, which assume the names of the constellations, comprise a Great Year of astrology which lasts about 25,000 years, with each of the ages lasting a little over 2000 years.

The ages of the existence of the human race go back to the Age of Leo. Following that age were the Age of Cancer, then the Age of Gemini. These three ages covered a period of time from which few records survive beyond the book of Genesis and the discoveries of archaeology. The ages of prehistory ended with the Age of Gemini when writing began. Then came the ages of recorded history: the Age of Taurus, which was the era of the building of great monuments such as the pyramids; the Age of Aries, during which God called the Hebrew race to be His chosen people; and the present Age of Pisces, which has been the Christian era. The Age of

Aquarius is yet to come, a period of time which embodies the world's dream of a golden age.

The Precession of the Equinoxes

An astrological age is the period of time which is required for the point of the spring equinox, which is 0º Aries in the zodiac, to go backwards through a constellation. The backward motion is a phenomenon of nature that was discovered in 134 B.C. by the Greek mathematician Hipparchus. The phenomenon has been named the Precession of the Equinoxes. It is the result of the fact that each year as the point of the spring equinox travels along the ecliptic through the zodiac, and returns each year to its starting place of the year before, it never completes a full circle. Each year, because of a slight tilt of the earth's axis, the equinoctial point falls a little short of where it was the year before. Therefore, it is receding very slowly in a clockwise direction against the backdrop of the constellations, those starry pictures visible in the night sky.

The backward movement of the equinoctial point is made at the rate of about one degree every 72 years. Therefore, based on the present rate of the Precession of the Equinoxes, the Great Year of astrology is calculated to take about 25,920 years. The retrograde journey in front of each constellation averages a little over 2000 years. The sequence of the astrological ages proceeds with the same predictable clockwork precision with which the sun, moon, and planets travel through the signs of the zodiac as they orbit the sun.

A perfect understanding of the technicalities of the

Precession of the Equinoxes is not necessary to an understanding of the astrological ages. Nor is such an understanding necessary to comprehending the content and purpose of this book.

However, it is important to understand that the constellations and the signs of the zodiac are not the same thing, even though they bear the same names. The zodiac is an intangible circle banding the earth beyond and parallel to the equator. It begins with 0º Aries, followed by each of the twelve signs in order, each measuring 30 degrees along the circle and all of them totaling 360 degrees. The signs in order are Aries, Taurus, Gemini, Cancer, Leo, Virgo, Libra, Scorpio, Sagittarius, Capricorn, Aquarius, and Pisces. The zodiac is confined to the solar system. It is interpreted within the context of the solar system and the positions of the sun, moon, and planets.

The constellations, on the other hand, are far out in space and are observed beyond the solar system. Whereas the signs of the zodiac can be measured accurately along the ecliptic – or the sun's apparent path of the solar system, the divisions of the circle of constellations can not be ascertained exactly, since no definite point can be determined where one constellation ends and another begins. This is why the exact dates of the astrological ages can not be pinpointed accurately.

The Ages of Mankind

The astrological ages apply to the stars of our galaxy and are measured in sidereal or celestial time. The following approximate dates are assigned to them:

The Astrological Ages

Age of Leo	10,000 B.C. to 8000 B.C.
Age of Cancer	8000 B.C. to 6000 B.C.
Age of Gemini	6000 B.C. to 4000 B.C.
Age of Taurus	4000 B.C. to 2000 B.C.
Age of Aries	2000 B.C. to the time of Christ
Age of Pisces	From the time of Christ to the present
Age of Aquarius	Yet to come

The prehistoric ages offer a fascinating field for research and investigation. Many facts concerning them have been uncovered by archaeologists, and the scientists have assigned their own names to what are called the anthropological ages: the Old Stone Age or the Paleolithic Period, the Middle Stone Age or the Mesolithic Period, the New Stone Age or the Neolithic Period, the Bronze Age, and the Iron Age. There is a noteworthy correspondence between the anthropological ages, which define the stages in the development of mankind, and the astrological ages.

Neither the divisions between the anthropological ages nor those of the astrological ages are sharp lines in time. The end of one age begins to assume the characteristics of the forthcoming age, and the next age at its beginning retains some of the qualities of the previous age. Especially do the ages overlap in their stages of development in different parts of the earth. What astrology tells us about the astrological ages coincides remarkably with the discoveries of archaeology. There is also a remarkable correspondence between the anthropological and the astrological ages and the biblical narrative of the early chapters of the book of Genesis.

The Age of Leo

The Age of Leo was the period of time when the point of the spring equinox – where the equator and the ecliptic intersect – receded slowly against the backdrop of the constellation Leo. The constellation to the ancients made a picture of a lion.

There are certain words that describe the astrological sign Leo. The same words describe the Age of Leo, which dated from about 10,000 B.C. to about 8000 B.C.

creativity	joy	romance
pride	vitality	pleasure
regal	willful	dramatic

Leo is a fire sign ruled by the sun, and its symbol is the lion. These elements, too, figured in the Age of Leo.

The history of the human race goes back to about 10,000 B.C. In astrology this was the beginning of the Age of Leo, the period of an abundant earth. It was the Old Stone Age in anthropology, and the era of innocence in the Garden of Eden. It was the time of God's creation of *homo sapiens,* after a catastrophe which occurred between the beginning of all things in Genesis 1:1 and the restoration of the earth in Genesis 1:2. The earth again became green, lush, and inhabitable, the home of plant, animal, and human life.

The sign of Leo as well as the Age of Leo are characterized by creativity. The Age of Leo was ruled by the sun and its warmth, which kept the earth productive and beautiful. In the dawn of its new creation, the planet was a place of inexpressible beauty. The luxuriant plant life, the prolific animal life, the mild temperatures, the long life span of the people – all these were characteristic of that era. Throughout the Age of Leo the vestiges of the first glow of creation permeated the still idyllic post-Edenic world for as long as 2000 years.

Those early ancestors of ours left their traces for the archaeologists to read. The remnants of their bones in the Fertile Crescent and around the Mediterranean Sea have been dated at about 10,000 B.C. These early remains of the human race are different from those of prehistoric beings, which have been dated prior to and about 30,000 B.C. and placed anthropologically in the early Paleolithic or early Old Stone Age.

The New Stone Age, or the Age of Leo, began in Egypt and Mesopotamia. The tribespeople who moved about to hunt animals and gather wild plants for their food began to domesticate goats and dogs. Goat's milk as a food was discovered by archaeologists in 1947 on the fossil remains which dated from 8500 B.C. in Iran.

The book of Genesis supplies many of the details of *homo sapiens* and his early life and environment. The primordial earth of Genesis as a tropical and subtropical paradise is described by scientist and lecturer Dr. Emil Gaverluk. "The evidence is in that planet Earth was a fantastically rich, beautiful, perfect place for all kinds of plant, animal and human forms far more numerous than we have understood." This idea is presented in Dr. Gaverluk's *Did Genesis Man Conquer Space?* There were no searing heat, no bitter cold, no wastelands. The earth, covered with mist, was verdant and fruitful. Even after sin entered Eden, some time was required for transgression to take its toll of the earth's bounty. For many years the earth retained much of the fresh exotic beauty of the Edenic creation. It is estimated that during the Age of Leo the world's population rose to about three million.

Genesis and the Age of Leo

The first five chapters of the book of Genesis give many particulars about the world at that time and how the human race lived. As shepherds and farmers they were people comfortable outdoors in the subtropical climate. Some were herdsmen who lived in tents. Others were musicians, coppersmiths, and blacksmiths, *"... those who play the harp and flute... every craftsman in bronze and iron"* (Genesis 4:21-22).

People lived for a long time. They were larger, healthier, and smarter than we. For they were not far removed from their ancestors Adam and Eve, who were perfect human specimens. They were vegetarians who did not yet need to eat meat, for the earth still provided in their food all the nutrients their bodies required. *"...You shall eat the herb of the field"* (Genesis 3:18). Animals were used for altar sacrifices and clothing. *"For Adam and his wife the Lord God made tunics of skins and clothed them"* (Genesis 3:21). God apparently had instructed the first family to make animal sacrifices for sin. *"Abel (the son of Adam) brought of the firstlings of his flock..."* (Genesis 4:4).

The people of that world, living for centuries, passed on their accumulated and shared knowledge to succeeding generations. The Greek philosopher Plato

Ruins of Jericho

Jericho, five miles west of the Jordan River and seven miles north of the Dead Sea, is probably the oldest city in the world. It is also the most excavated, with five layers of towns uncovered by the archaeologists.

The earliest settlement was a pre-pottery Neolithic town, dating to 8000 B.C., the Age of Leo or Cancer. The excavated town was protected by strong walls. Within them were mud brick and stone houses containing clay figures of animals and goddesses, reed mats, and plastered floors.

English, German, and American archaeologists have worked on Jericho digs since 1908.

The modern city of Jericho is a popular winter resort, and its tropical climate makes it a year-round source of vegetables and fruit, in spite of Joshua the Hebrew warrior's curse: "*...Cursed be the man...who rises up and builds this city Jericho...*" (Joshua 6:26).

described a similarly idyllic place called Atlantis, a legendary land unsurpassed in beauty and power. Plato dated Atlantis at 9500 B.C., contemporary with the period called in astrology the Age of Leo. That age, due to subsequent destruction, is primarily a lost era as far as relics and records are concerned. There remain only traces as to clues concerning the heights the human race attained in that long ago time. But later civilizations would bear the marks of a common ancestral culture, the obscure heritage of the Age of Leo.

The Age of Leo ended in catastrophe. The knowledge of God which had been handed down from Adam, Seth, and Enoch, by the end of the age was distorted in a number of ways. Among the heathen it became an age of sun worship. As a witness, the ancient temples of South America, dedicated to the sun, bear the carved faces of lions, symbolic of the astrological sign of Leo, whose ruler is the sun.

Religion was distorted into a worship of half-gods and half-men. From various sources there have come to us tales of adventure and leonine romance. Plato wrote of the ancient supermen and heroes of Atlantis. The Greek poets described inventive men who were half-gods. And Genesis agrees with the existence of giants and heroes. *"There were giants on the earth in those days, and also afterward, when the sons of God came in to the daughters of men, and they bore children to them. Those were the mighty men who were of old, men of renown"* (Genesis 6:4-5). The Bible says that it was the sinfulness of these people over the earth which brought the doom of that glorious age. Their actions had degenerated from the original instructions from God.

The narrative in Genesis explains, *"Then the Lord saw that the wickedness of man was great in the earth, and that every intent of the thoughts of his heart was only evil continually. And the Lord was sorry that He had made man on the earth, and He was grieved in his heart. So the Lord said, 'I will destroy man whom I have created from the face of the earth, both man and beast, creeping thing and birds of the air, for I am sorry that I have made them'"* (Genesis 6:5-7). So the age brought its own destruction, as sin took its toll of the earth, and the Age of Leo passed with the deluge of the watery Age of Cancer.

The Age of Cancer

The Age of Cancer was the period of time when the point of the spring equinox – where the equator and the ecliptic intersect – receded slowly against the backdrop of the constellation Cancer. The constellation to the ancients made a picture of a crab.

There are certain words that describe the astrological sign Cancer. The same words describe the Age of Cancer, which dated from about 8000 B.C. to about 6000 B.C.

land	mother	home
family	nurture	compassion
changeable	sensitive	protective

Cancer is a water sign ruled by the moon, and its symbol is the crab. These elements, too, figured in the Age of Cancer.

The Age of Cancer began about 8000 B.C. and lasted approximately 2000 years. Cancer is a water sign, and appropriately the most notable event of that age was the great flood of Noah's day in Mesopotamia. Legends of a deluge and the miraculous escape of a handful of survivors are universal from Babylonia to the Western Hemisphere. Later Sumerian cuneiform writing in the earliest known written legend would tell of a great flood in which the human race was saved by the building of an ark.

There is a distinguishing factor in the Hebrew story in Genesis of Noah and his family who survived the flood, which sets it apart from the others. It is the narrative's inclusion of the working out of the purposes of God both in the deluge itself and in the events which followed. The story is familiar to most readers. Noah, being the only good man of his time, was told by God to build an ark in which to save himself and his family.

Noah's Ark

Noah's instructions were to take into the ark his family, along with seven pairs of all ritually clean animals, one pair of every unclean animal and seven pairs of every bird. When all these were safely inside the ark, on the seventeenth day of the second month Marchessan (November), the rains came for forty days and forty nights. At this time the ark began to float upon the water. The rain continued for 150 days, and all living things on the earth were destroyed. Then the waters began to subside.

On the seventeenth day of the seventh month Nisan (April), the ark landed on a mountain in Ararat. The water receded until the first day of the tenth month Tammuz (July), when land could be seen. On the first

Noah's Ark

In the biblical account Noah's ark rode the waters of the Great Deluge of the Age of Cancer for eleven months. The rains began in the second month of Noah's six hundred and first year of life. He emerged from the ark in the first month of his six hundred and second year.

Most civilizations have legends of a great flood, indicating a common cultural heritage from a distant past.

A fragment of a clay tablet excavated from the library of Ashurbanipal at Nineveh gives the Assyrian account of a flood in the region of Mesopotamia.

A Sumarian King List on fragment tablets dug up by archaeologists in 1906 tells about eight ante-diluvian rulers. Its phrase "before the flood" shows literal acceptance of the flood.

The stylized ark in the photograph is from a stained glass window in the former First Baptist Church building in Charlotte, North Carolina, now an arts center.

day of the first month Tishri (October), Noah opened the hatch of the ark and looked out on dry land. After a year and ten days in the ark, on the twenty-seventh day of the second month Marchessan (November), Noah came out of the ark with his family and all the animals. His first act was to build an altar to the Lord.

God made a promise to Noah. Never again would He destroy all the inhabitants of the earth by flood. *"'... I will never again curse the ground for man's sake... nor will I again destroy every living thing, as I have done. While the earth remains, seedtime and harvest, and cold and heat, and winter and summer, day and night, shall not cease'"* (Genesis 8:21-22). This is the first mention of cold and winter in the Bible. The warm weather of the Age of Leo was past, and mankind now truly lived in the Age of Cancer.

Flavius Josephus, Jewish historian, in his *Antiquities,* Chapter III, wrote that the flood began "two thousand six hundred and fifty-six years from Adam, the first man; and the time is written down in our sacred books, those who then lived having noted down, with great accuracy, both the births and deaths of illustrious men." Josephus no doubt used genealogies available to him but which were later lost and certainly are lost to us today. The calculations of Josephus concerning the time from Adam to the flood agree with the accepted lengths of the astrological ages of Leo and Cancer.

After the Ark

The sign of Cancer is the sign of fertility and fecundity. One of the specific instructions given by God to Noah and his family was appropriately to replenish the earth.

Snow-capped Alps

The Swiss Alps above as seen from Mount Titlis are an extreme of cold and beauty. The first mention of the cold and winter, heat and summer in the Bible came after the flood in the Age of Cancer. They were in the promise that God made to Noah, *"...The Lord said in His heart, 'I will never again curse the ground...nor will I again destroy every living thing as I have done.*

"While the earth remains
Seedtime and harvest,
And cold and heat,
And winter and summer,
And day and night
Shall not cease'"
(Genesis 8:21,22)

God told Noah, his three sons, and their wives to multiply. *"...Be fruitful and multiply; bring forth abundantly in the earth and multiply in it'"* (Genesis 9:7). Noah's family obeyed and increased. Their genealogies are listed in Genesis 10. *"There were the families of the sons of Noah, according to their generations, in their nations; and from these the nations were divided on the earth after the flood"* (Genesis 10:32). During the Age of Cancer the earth's population reached an estimated five million.

Another instruction given to Noah's family was to eat meat, this being the first time mankind was ever told to eat the flesh of animals. *"Every moving thing that lives shall be food for you. I have given you all things, even the green herbs"* (Genesis 9:3). No longer was the soil alone able to provide full nourishment for people. Life would be harder; the life span would be shorter. After generations of living for centuries, as did Adam, Seth, Enoch, and Methuselah, people now were to have their life span reduced. *"... The Lord said, '... His days shall be one hundred and twenty years'"* (Genesis 6:3).

The lifestyle of people drastically changed. They became nomads whose primary quest was to acquire food. They transported their tents to new places where food could be found, just as the hermit crab, the symbol of Cancer, carries his house on his back. The Cancerian age like the Age of Leo can be identified with the Neolithic or New Stone Age period. Village farmers began to replace food-gathering tribespeople. As the people began to farm, to plant vineyards and orchards, and to domesticate animals in the Near East and in Mesopotamia, their lives became more stable.

There appeared the small towns of the Neolithic

Period: Jericho in the Jordan Valley, Jarmo in northeast Mesopotamia, and Hassuna west of the Tigris River. Archaeologists have dated these excavated villages from 10,000 B.C. to 5000 B.C. Jericho was a settlement north of the Dead Sea with a population of 2500 in the middle of the Age of Cancer. Archaeologists have uncovered layers of cities built on the same spot. In the Age of Cancer it was a walled town. A team of archaeologists in 1948 A.D. unearthed the Kurdistan village of Jarmo which was founded during the Age of Cancer, one of the first permanent agricultural settlements.

Then people forgot God again. Traces of moon-cults and female fertility goddesses date back to the Age of Cancer, whose sign is ruled by the moon. So it is seen that it did not take long for the new population of the earth to depart again from pure religion. Again, the creature began to worship the creation rather than the Creator. Nowhere is this more vividly portrayed than in the story of the Tower of Babel of the next age, the Age of Gemini.

The Age of Gemini

The Age of Gemini was the period of time when the point of the spring equinox – where the equator and the ecliptic intersect – receded slowly against the backdrop of the constellation Gemini. The constellation to the ancients made a picture of twin boys.

There are certain words that describe the astrological sign Gemini. The same words describe the Age of Gemini, which dated from about 6000 B.C. to about 4000 B.C.

communication	learning	duality
versatility	intellect	mobility
expressive	divisive	adaptable

Gemini is an air sign ruled by Mercury, and its symbol is the twin boys. These elements, too, figured in the Age of Gemini.

By astrological timekeeping the Age of Gemini dated from about 6000 B.C. to approximately 4000 B.C. Mankind's written record began with the Age of Gemini. From that time to the present people have left an indelible story. Their saga has been told in stone, on metal, in the building of monuments, on parchment and paper. Some branches of Christians place the date of Creation in the Age of Gemini. In the seventh century A.D., the year 5508 B.C. in the Age of Gemini was adopted as the Year of Creation by the Eastern Orthodox Church. The year 5490 B.C. in the Age of Gemini was selected as the Year of Creation by the early Syrian Christians.

During the Age of Gemini, as the survivors of the great deluge and their descendants continued to repopulate the Fertile Crescent and beyond, they also stretched their intellectual horizons. Their most noteworthy involvement was in the area of the spoken and written word. Just as Gemini is the astrological sign of language, so the Age of Gemini was the age of language, for as always the characteristics of the astrological sign and the development of the astrological age go hand in hand.

Another of the intellectual accomplishments of the human mind during this period was in the field of astronomy or astrology, which were then one and the same. People increased their knowledge of the heavens to the extent that over widespread locations they built great observatories in order to measure better the movements of the celestial bodies. In Mesopotamia giant towers called ziggurats were erected, with gardened terraces ascending their walls and observatories topping their summits. From these pinnacles the courses of the stars and planets could be accurately plotted, and the eclipses of the sun and moon were predicted. The most famous of the ziggurats was the Tower of Babel on the plain of Shinar.

The Tower of Babel

Genesis tells the story with an account given from God's own perspective and action, concerning His condemnation of the human race for worshipping the creature and the creation rather than the One who made them. *"Now the whole earth had one language and one speech. And it came to pass, as they journeyed from the east, that they found a plain in the land of Shinar, they dwelt there. Then they said to one another, 'Come, let us make bricks and bake them thoroughly.' They had brick for stone, and they had asphalt for mortar. And they said, 'Come, let us build ourselves a city, and a tower whose top is in the heavens; let us make a name for ourselves lest we shall be scattered abroad over the face of the whole earth.' But the Lord came down to see the city and the tower which the sons of men had built. And the Lord said, 'Indeed the people are one and they all have one language, and this is what they begin to do; now nothing that they propose to do will be withheld from them. Come, let Us go down and there confuse their language that they may not understand one another's speech.' So the Lord scattered them abroad from there over the face of the earth and they ceased building the city. Therefore its name is called Babel, because there the Lord confused the language of all the earth; and from there the Lord scattered them abroad over the face of the earth"* (Genesis 11:1-9).

During the Age of Gemini distinct language groups were established throughout the areas that are now Asia, Africa, and Europe: the Semitic, Hamitic, Sumerian, Hurrian, and Indo-European groups. Many of these peoples were still wanderers, seeking hunting or grazing grounds. But by 5000 B.C. in the middle of the Age of Gemini villages began to cluster. The Age of Gemini was also the age of written language, first pictographs and hieroglyphics in stone and then cuneiform writing on clay tablets. Today one views the displays of Egyptian hieroglyphics inscribed on stone monuments and marvels at their intricacies.

Other Geminian matters flourished. The age whose ruler Gemini is the sign of learning, communication, and transportation, spawned the introduction of the wheel and the cart. The wheel, invented by Sumerians in the Tigris-Euphrates Basin, hastened the development of transportation, faster travel, warfare, industry, and construction. Artisans in Persia smelted a soft copper that could be molded and shaped. In the Fertile Crescent a need for water sometimes led to warfare between villages. There and in Egypt canals were built.

Progress accelerated. Horses were domesticated. The Swiss lake dwellers used the strong fibers of wild flax to

Levi Window by Chagall

In the synagogue of the Hadassah-Hebrew University Medical Center in Jerusalem are twelve stained glass windows by Marc Chagall. Each one of the windows represents one of the tribes of Israel.

Jewish religious law does not permit the reproduction of a likeness of a human being. The Chagall windows, therefore, picture animals, plants, and parts of the physical universe.

The yellow window on the right in the photograph depicts the tribe of Levi, which Jewish astrologers have believed is the Gemini tribe. The dual nature of the sign Gemini and of the Age of Gemini is apparent in the window.

In the Levi window the Gemini nature is shown in the pairs of birds and animals. The double tablet depicts Gemini writing, language, and learning. The Hebrew words are translated, *"They shall teach Jacob thy judgements, and Israel thy law..."* (Deuteronomy 33:10).

make lines and nets for fishing, and ropes and cords for building construction and navigation. The first true pottery was made, introducing new methods of cooking. Corn and beans were grown in the Western Hemisphere. People congregated in cities and began to keep records of their business and political affairs. A calendar was devised with months, hours, and minutes. The geometric circle was divided into 360 degrees. A system of weights and measures was invented.

Gemini is a double sign, whose symbol is the twins. Many of the events of the Age of Gemini dealt with divisions and pairs. In Genesis the twin nature of the age is recorded. *"To Eber were born two sons: the name of one was Peleg, for in his days the earth was divided; and his brother's name was Joktan"* (Genesis 10:25). The name Peleg means Division. This verse may indicate that this was the time when the continents broke apart from each other, perhaps the result of a cataclysmic event.

During the Geminian age Egypt became a twin civilization with two great centers, Noph (Memphis) and No-Amon (Thebes), which alternated as capital cities of the dual kingdom. The people worshipped two Nile gods. It was not until the next age around 3000 B.C. that Upper Egypt and Lower Egypt were united, this occurring only after the dual age of Gemini had given way to the Age of Taurus.

The Age of Taurus

The Age of Taurus was the period of time when the point of the spring equinox – where the equator and the ecliptic intersect – receded slowly against the backdrop of the constellation Taurus. The constellation to the ancients made a picture of a bull.

There are certain words that describe the astrological sign Taurus. The same words describe the Age of Taurus, which dated from about 4000 B.C. to 2000 B.C.

property	finance	strength
artistry	tastefulness	construction
possessive	practical	enduring

Taurus is an earth sign ruled by Venus, and its symbol is the bull. These elements, too, figured in the Age of Taurus.

The astrological Age of Taurus, lasting approximately from 4000 B.C. to 2000 B.C., corresponded to the anthropological period of the latter part of the New Stone Age and the beginning of the Bronze Age. The Age of Taurus extended well into the period of recorded history, and the investigator of this age discovers an abundance of records and relics. No longer must one rely on educated guesses.

Sumer, which is generally considered to be the first full-blown human civilization, developed in the valleys of the Tigris and Euphrates Rivers. Annual floods deposited fresh layers of fertile soil for use by the agricultural tribespeople. The Sumerians settled in communities, which evolved with administrative systems governed by priests. The Sumerians reached the pinnacle of their development in the Age of Taurus. They had wheeled vehicles drawn by animals and oar-powered ships, the beginning of which had appeared

The Great Pyramid at Giza

This pyramid at Giza, Egypt, was built during the Age of Taurus. The over two million polished limestone blocks weigh two or three tons each. They are shown here near the pyramid's entrance.

In 1925 the Egyptian government made accurate measurements of the pyramid. The lengths of the four sides vary by less than eight inches. The sides are aligned with the cardinal points of the compass, and at the winter solstice make no shadows.

Explorers of the pyramids in the seventeenth through the nineteenth centuries concluded that the ancient Egyptians possessed advanced geometrical information, knew the circumference of the earth, the distance from the center of the earth to the poles, and the value of pi. They considered this evidence that much of ancient knowledge has been lost.

Napoleon Bonaparte's soldiers, attempting to explore the interior of the Great Pyramid, were driven off by scratching, smelly bats. Napoleon himself is supposed to have entered the pyramid and emerged white-faced and shaken, but he never told anybody why.

in the former Age of Gemini. The people of this region which is now southeastern Iraq flourished from 3500 B.C. to 2000 B.C. The scientists have dug up an abundance of their work in metal and stone – jewelry, pottery, armor, and weapons. Their cuneiform writing on clay tablets and stone have also rewarded the archaeologists.

The Age of Taurus was a time of vast building. Taurus is the astrological sign of endurance and solidity. The engineering and mathematics developed during the Age of Gemini served well the massive construction of the Taurean age, and characteristically the Age of Taurus built its monuments to last. At that time were built the great pyramids of Egypt, the mysterious Stonehenge, and the temples of ancient Mexico and Peru. It is of great interest to the astrologer that these structures were built with many astrological and astronomical connotations. Stonehenge near Salisbury, England, a circle of great monoliths or single stones, was laid out so that certain of the stones were aligned with the rising sun on the days of the summer and winter solstices.

Likewise the Great Pyramid of Egypt, built on the border between the old kingdoms of Upper and Lower Egypt in the center of Egypt, had astronomical implications. The cornerstones at the four bases of the Great Pyramid of Giza point due east, west, north, and south, and at the time of the change to the spring and autumn equinoxes, there are no shadows on any side of the structure. The Great Sphinx was carved from rock at Giza, 240 feet long. The four parts of the Sphinx – the human head, the body of a lion, the wings of an eagle, and the hooves of a bull – represent the four fixed signs of the zodiac: Aquarius, Leo, Scorpio, and Taurus.

The Great Sphinx

The Sphinx at Giza is the largest and best known. It is carved of limestone, 240 feet long and 66 feet high. For many years the Sphinx, except for its head, lay buried under the sand.

Napoleon fought the Egyptians at the Battle of the Pyramids, near the Sphinx. The story goes that the Sphinx lost its nose when the conqueror's soldiers used it for target practice.

The Sphinx has astrological significance, representing the four fixed signs of the zodiac: the human head (Aquarius), the body of an ox (Taurus), the wings of an eagle (Scorpio), and the legs and paws of a lion (Leo). A sphinx carved later by the Greeks had a woman's head, a lion's body, wings, and a serpent's tail. Archaeologists have found sphinxes in ancient Assyria and Phoenicia. Sphinxes were used as guardians of religious places, reminiscent of the cherubim guarding the Garden of Eden. This suggests a common cultural heritage among all people.

During this age the step Pyramid at Sakkara in Egypt was built. Egypt's First Dynasty began when Upper and Lower Egypt were united under the pharoah Menes. He expanded the city of Memphis.

It is estimated that during the Age of Taurus the world's population reached 100 million.

Artifacts of Taurus

Taurus is not only the astrological sign of strength, but also the sign of beauty. In 3600 B.C. bronze, the first hard metal, was made from copper alloyed with tin. Characteristic of the Taurean earth sign, the Age of Taurus brought an increase in mining operations and the smelting of iron ore. Some astrologers believe that the lost planet Vulcan rather than Venus is the true ruler of the sign Taurus, and in Greek and Roman mythology the god Vulcan was depicted as a forger of metal. The Taurean metal work was typical of the Bronze Age culture, for people were using ax heads made of bronze, and the Sumerians in particular were wearing bronze armor.

The Age of Taurus, again typical of the fixed sign Taurus, was one of stability. Land was important. Canals were dug to irrigate farmlands, and with the permanence of farming came permanent villages, well constructed and well fortified. Over for the most part were the wanderings of the Age of Gemini.

The walls and the public buildings of the cities exhibited another Taurean accomplishment – the arts. The Taurean love for beautiful objects is seen in the excavated relics of metal, gold, and precious stones, articles of personal adornment, paintings, and statuettes. The Age of Taurus brought the flowering of both art and architecture.

Among the public buildings of the Taurean age were the great libraries which held the treasures of the ages. They housed the books and scrolls which had followed the invention of writing, including the heroic epics produced by the story tellers of nearly all the civilizations. Myth making was the obsession of the age. It is interesting that the myths among the various peoples of the earth contained certain similarities. This is evidence not that they copied each other but that they all shared a common religious and cultural heritage from a distant past.

The religions of the Age of Taurus often displayed the symbol of the sign Taurus, the bull. There were the rites of the Sacred Bull of Assyria, the worship of the golden calf of Egypt, and the Winged Bull of Phoenicia. Their images were made in bronze and gold, symbolizing the strength, vigor, and endurance of the sign of Taurus and of the Age of Taurus. That age as a period of farming furnished the circumstance for the emergence of the fabricated gods of fertility and agriculture. Among them were the god Marduk and his female counterpart.

It is necessary to say here, because of the widely held opinion, that many students of the Bible believe that the story of the human species is about 6000 years old instead of the 12,000 years set forth in this book. By this reckoning the creation of Adam and Eve would have taken place about 4000 B.C. near the beginning of the Age of Taurus, and all the events of the first eleven chapters of Genesis to the time of Abraham would have occurred during that age.

This view is held by many competent Bible scholars. The Irish theologian James Ussher in 1650 A.D. reckoned the year 4004 B.C. near the beginning of the Age of Taurus to be the date of creation. This is still a popular belief. For other opinions, the Hebrew Calendar from the fifteenth century A.D. used the year 3760 B.C. in the Age of Taurus as the Year of Creation, while the Mayan calendars in the Western Hemisphere used 3641 B.C. also in the Age of Taurus. Take your pick. Our pick is approximately 10,000 B.C. as the date for the appearance of *homo sapiens*. This gives six ages of human history, with the seventh age the coming Millenium.

The Bible is largely silent concerning the events of the Age of Taurus. The people of the earth during this age were building their great civilizations in preparation for the Age of Aries. The 12th chapter of Genesis resumes the narrative with the story of Abraham the patriarch and the beginning of the Age of Aries.

Chapter 3

The Age of Aries

The Age of Aries was the period of time when the point of the spring equinox – where the equator and the ecliptic intersect – receded slowly against the backdrop of the constellation Aries. The constellation to the ancients made a picture of a ram.

There are certain words that describe the astrological sign Aries. The same words describe the Age of Aries, which dated from about 2000 B.C. to the time of Christ.

selfhood	leadership	energy
enthusiasm	activity	initiative
aggressive	combative	outgoing

Aries is a fire sign ruled by Mars, and its symbol is the ram. These elements, too, figured in the Age of Aries.

In the Bible the Age of Aries extended from the time of Abraham to the time of Christ. In regard to religion, the most notable development of the age was the calling out of the Hebrews to become God's chosen people. In respect to prophecy, a great prophecy of Daniel concerned the kingdoms of the world from his own time to the end of time. It constitutes, in the view of many, the most astounding single prophecy every made.

Most of the Old Testament was encompassed within the Age of Aries, the era of the ram and the sacrificial lamb. The age began with the patriarch Abraham. Abraham's father, Terah, was descended from Shem the son of Noah, one of the three sons of Noah who were

Mamre

Mamre, one of the stops on Abraham's meanderings through Canaan when he first came from the Fertile Crescent near the beginning of the Age of Aries, is now occupied territory near Hebron. It was at Mamre that Abraham first received God's promise that his descendants would inherit the land forever.

Archaeologists have excavated some of the cities Abraham visited – Shechem, Bethel, Hebron, and Beer-Sheba – and have found them to have been thriving Middle Bronze Age centers.

Canaan was important as the crossroads of three continents – Asia, Africa, and Europe. It served as a highway for the caravans of traders and the armies of conquerers.

At Mamre, Abraham dwelt near the terebinth trees, whose roots can go 200 feet below the surface of the desert to reach water.

told in the Age of Cancer to replenish the earth. *"So God blessed Noah and his sons, and said to them, 'Be fruitful and multiply, and fill the earth'"* (Genesis 9:1).

The Patriarch Abraham

Through the age of Gemini and the Age of Taurus the descendants of Shem repopulated the region of the Fertile Crescent. Around the year 2000 B.C. near the beginning of the Age of Aries, Terah left the city of Ur in Babylonia, a site which is now in Iraq. The thriving metropolis of Ur was excavated by archaeologists in 1934, revealing the magnificence of structures and commerce in the Ages of Taurus and Aries. Leaving the flourishing port city, Terah took his family – including Abraham – to Haran, a location which is now in Syria.

After Terah died, the Lord called Abraham to go to Canaan, a land on the Mediterranean coast which is now the state of Israel. Abraham obeyed, traveling to Canaan with his considerable number of possessions and servants. With his wife Sarah he journeyed, building an altar and making the sacrifice of a ram to the Lord on all the stops along the way. He came to Shechem and made an altar, then to a mountain near Bethel where he built another altar. He made a sojourn to Egypt, then returned to the altar at Bethel.

God spoke to Abraham and promised him all the land as far as he could see. After the promise, the patriarch moved to where the terebinth trees grew at Mamre in Hebron. He built his altar and dwelt there. At Mamre the Lord made a surprising prophecy to Abraham.

The Lord asked him to bring a three-year-old ram and

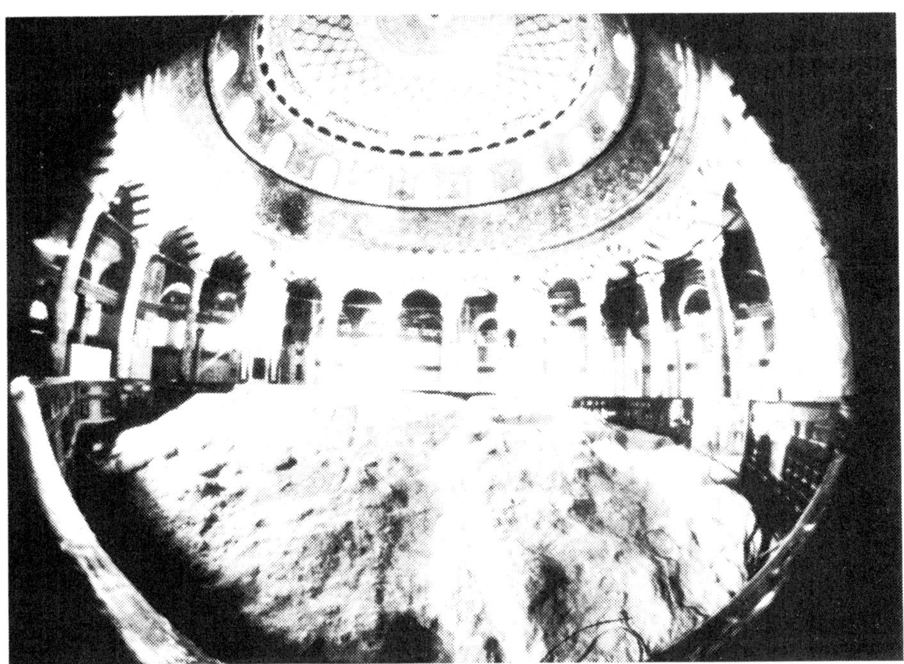

The Rock of Abraham

The rock of Abraham is Mount Moriah itself, an integral part of the top of the mountain. It is the rock where Abraham was willing to sacrifice his son Isaac, and the threshing floor which King David purchased during the Age of Aries to be the site of Solomon's Temple.

Today the rock is inside the Islamic Dome of the Rock and is the centerpiece of the mosque. The rock is enclosed by an iron grille. Still visible are the holes bored for drainage when the rock was the altar of the burnt offerings of the ram in the Temple. Because the rock was part of the mountain, it was not destroyed by the Babylonians in 586 B.C. or by the Romans in A.D. 70. Its surface, worn smooth by tourists' fingers, can be touched through the iron fence.

other animals to the altar, and when this was done, God prophesied to Abraham, "*...Know certainly that your descendants will be strangers in a land that is not theirs, and will serve them, and they will afflict them for four hundred years....Afterward they shall come out with great possessions*" (Genesis 15:13,14). When the sun went down, a burning torch passed between the pieces of the ram and the other meat on the altar. This prophecy was fulfilled after the death of Abraham during the lifetime of his grandson Jacob and his great-grandsons, when the Hebrews began a stretch of 400 years as slaves in Egypt.

It was on the mountain of Moriah – which would later become the site of the holy city Jerusalem – that Abraham sacrificed a ram which the Lord provided. "*Abraham looked, and there behind him was a ram caught in a thicket by its horns. So Abraham took the ram and offered it up for a burnt offering...*" (Genesis 22:13). This was early in the Age of Aries.

The Kingdoms of the Fertile Crescent

Between the time of Abraham and Daniel the true militant nature of the age was evident. Nations grew and overturned other nations. Empires absorbed weaker peoples around them and subjugated their populations, often making slaves of them and sometimes deporting them. Sumer, the civilization between the Tigris and Euphrates rivers, which had reached the ascendancy during the Age of Taurus, experienced constant warfare, and was finally weakened by hostile attacks.

About 1760 B.C. the great warrior Hammurabi conquered the region of Mesopotamia and established the Old Babylonian Empire. This kingdom is to be distinguished from the New Babylonian Empire of Daniel's time. Hammurabi described himself as "Mighty King, King of Babylon, King of the whole country of Amurru, King of Sumer and Akkad, King of the Four Quarters of the world." His empire had magnificent palaces, temples, and private houses. Commerce flourished in Babylon, and the city was an important political and cultural power.

Hammurabi died in 1750 B.C., and in 1660 B.C. Babylon was sacked by the warring Hittites from the west. Then a mountain group – the Kassites – overpowered the Hittites and ruled for 400 years. In 1150 the empire was raided by the Elamites and then by the warlike Assyrians from the north area of the Fertile Crescent. Power in combat was now centered in the use of two-wheeled horse-drawn chariots and the latest iron weapons.

Old Babylon was destroyed in 689 B.C. by the Assyrian king Sennacherib and the population slaughtered. Sennacherib conquered most of Syria and Palestine, and much of Egypt. The Assyrians' cruelty is pictured in their own carvings. Revolts against them were savagely crushed. The warlike tendencies of the Age of Aries were at their height. The anthropological Iron Age was in full sway.

The Assyrian dominance of Mesopotamia ended with their defeat by Nabopolasser, who ruled Babylon from 626 B.C. to 605 B.C. His son Nebuchadnezzar II inherited the throne and continued to rebuild Babylon to its state of grandeur which the city enjoyed when the prophet Daniel became a captive there.

In his own writings Nebuchadnezzar did not give as much importance to his military exploits as he did to his building projects. He rebuilt the magnificent city of Babylon, which German archaeologists excavated from 1899 to 1917, uncovering the city's massive walls and elegant palaces and temples. He constructed the Hanging Gardens of Babylon on rooftops, which were one of the Seven Wonders of the Ancient World.

The Hebrews

Meanwhile in the land of Canaan the events of the Age of Aries had had their impact on the Israelites. When Joseph – the son of Jacob and the great-grandson of Abraham – was sold into slavery in Egypt, he did what Daniel was later to do in Babylon. He interpreted dreams and thereby gained the favor of the pharoah. When his brothers, during a famine in Canaan, came to Egypt in search of food, they stayed there and so did their descendants for 400 years. This fulfilled the prophecy given to Abraham.

Egyptian supremacy at this time was recognized even by Old Babylonia. The pharoahs ruled for 1000 miles along the Nile River and launched great building programs at Karnak and Luxor. Forced Israelite labor was used to build the great Egyptian cities Pithon and Ramses. Soon Moses led the exodus of the Hebrews from Egypt, and on their way to Canaan presented them with the Ten Commandments and the Mosaic Law. The Old Babylonian Empire rose in the Fertile Crescent while the Israelites fought the Canaanites for land. Then Babylonia fell again before the Assyrians.

The Exodus from Egypt

Jacob's family, from whom all Hebrews are descended, numbered 75 when they went into Egypt during a famine to find food. *"Then Joseph sent and called his father Jacob and all his relatives to him, seventy-five people. So Jacob went down to Egypt..."* (Acts 7:14,15). When they came out, they were a great nation, numbering 600,000 men. *"Then the children of Israel journeyed from Rameses to Succoth, about six hundred thousand men on foot, besides children"* (Exodus 12:37).

Rameses II was the probable pharaoh of the Exodus. His successor, Pharaoh Merneptah, left a stele which was discovered by archaeologists at Thebes, and which is called the Israel Tablet. The cunieform tablet is dated about 1229 B.C., and mentions the departure of the Israelites from Egypt.

The tall palm trees in the photograph above grow along the Mediterranean coast, along the most direct route from the city of Rameses to Gaza in Canaan. The Israelites took a longer – and safer – journey out of the land of their bondage, with Moses leading them.

While the Assyrians expanded their territory, the Golden Age of the Hebrew Monarchy flourished under the kings, Saul, David, and Solomon. When the country split after the death of Solomon, the Assyrians plagued both the Northern and Southern Kingdoms. As the Assyrians swept over the land to the Mediterranean Sea, Israel felt the heel of the Iron Age. The Northern Kingdom was conquered and the people deported and scattered in 721 B.C.

King Nebuchadnezzar

Supremacy again had changed hands in the Fertile Crescent, as the New Babylonian Empire took the ascendancy of world power from the Assyrians. Ninevah, the Assyrian capital, was defeated by the Medes and the Chaldeans, and the Hebrew Southern Kingdom in Judea faced the Babylonian threat.

King Nebuchadnezzar II made three devastating attacks on Judah. Jerusalem fell to the Babylonian king in 597 B.C. Ten years later in 587 B.C., the Babylonians deported a group of Israelites, including the young man Daniel, and brought them to the remarkable city of Babylon in the Fertile Crescent. The Temple in Jerusalem was destroyed by the Babylonians in 586 B.C.

The best of the Israelites were taken to Babylon in the deportation of the Hebrews from Judea to the land on the Euphrates River. It was during this exile that the Hebrews acquired the name Jews, from the fact that they were from Judea. As the exiles were oriented to a new and vastly different culture from that of Judea, the choicest among them were installed in the king's palace.

Daniel, because he had the gift of interpreting dreams, pleased the king. He rose to a position of power in Babylon. He was an administrator of public affairs when King Nebuchadnezzar had the dream of all dreams.

Desiring an interpretation of his strange dream, the king went to the soothsayers, the magicians, and the astrologers of his realm. The book of Daniel does not make it conclusively clear whether the king had forgotten the dream which continued to trouble him, or whether he was deliberately concealing it in order to test the accuracy of any forthcoming interpretation. In either case, the king demanded that the wise men of his kingdom tell him what the dream had been and what it meant.

The Prophet Daniel

When they failed to do so, Nebuchadnezzar threatened their lives, and in fear they turned to Daniel, who was also under the death threat. Daniel went to the king and asked for time to arrive at an interpretation of the dream. When the request was granted, Daniel and his Hebrew companions prayed to the God of the Hebrews. They prayed to *"seek mercies from the God of heaven concerning this secret, so that Daniel and his companions might not perish with the rest of the wise men of Babylon"* (Daniel 2:18).

In a night vision the secret of the dream was revealed to Daniel. After receiving the meaning of the king's dream, Daniel voiced in poetry his prayer of thanksgiving to God:

"Blessed be the name of God forever and ever,

For wisdom and might are his.
And he changes the times and the seasons;
He removes kings and raises up kings;
He gives wisdom to the wise
And knowledge to those who have understanding.
He reveals deep and secret things;
He knows what is in the darkness,
And light dwells with Him.

"I thank You and praise You,
O God of my fathers;
You have given me wisdom and might,
And have now made known to me what
we asked of You,
For You have made known to us the King's demand"
(Daniel 2:20-23).

Then Daniel went to the king's deputy and said, "*...Do not destroy the wise men of Babylon; take me before the king, and I will tell the king the interpretation*" (Daniel 2:24).

Brought to the king, Daniel said to him, "*The secret which the king has demanded, the wise men, the astrologers, the magicians, and the soothsayers cannot declare to the king. But there is a God in heaven who reveals secrets, and He has made known to King Nebuchadnezzar what will be in the latter days. Your dream, and the visions of your head upon your bed were these*" (Daniel 2:27,28).

Nebuchadnezzar's Dream

First Daniel told the king why he had had the dream. "*As for you, O king, thoughts came to your mind while on your bed, about what would come to pass after this; and He who reveals secrets has made known to you what will be"* (Daniel 2:29).

The king wanted to know the future, and his desire was to be granted. Daniel's description of the dream and the interpretation of it would tell King Nebuchadnezzar the coming events of both the near and far future.

Daniel said, *"You, O king, were watching; and behold a great image! This great image, whose splendor was excellent, stood before you and its form was awesome. This image's head was of fine gold, its chest and arms of silver, its belly and thighs of bronze, its legs of iron, its feet partly of iron and partly of clay"* (Daniel 2:31-33).

Then Daniel described to the king what would happen to the image. *"You watched while a stone was cut out without hands, which struck the image on its feet of iron and clay, and broke them in pieces. Then the iron, the clay, the bronze, the silver, and the gold were crushed together, and became like chaff from the summer threshing floors; the wind carried them away so that no trace of them was found. And the stone that struck the image became a great mountain and filled the whole earth. This is the dream..."* (Daniel 2:34-36).

The Head of Gold

Daniel said, *"...Now we will tell the interpretation of it before the king"* (Daniel 2:36). Daniel, as he began the interpretation of the dream, exercised superb diplomacy in addressing the king. *"You, O king, are a king of kings. For the God of heaven has given you a kingdom, power, strength, and glory; and wherever the children of men dwell, or the beasts of the field and the birds of heaven, He has given*

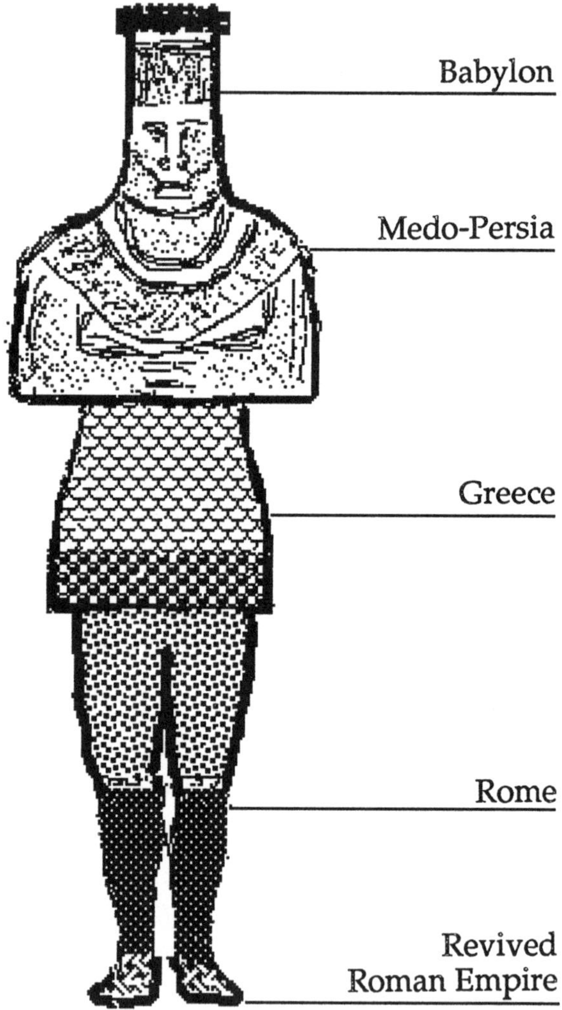

The Image
in
Nebuchadnezzar's Dream
Daniel 2

them into your hand, and has made you ruler over them all – you are this head of gold" (Daniel 2:37, 38).

The head of gold of the image in the king's dream was his own kingdom of Babylon. It was the empire which had dominated the world since 605 B.C. Babylon, however, in all its grandeur was not to endure.

The Chest of Silver

Daniel said to the king, *"But after you shall rise another kingdom inferior to yours..."* (Daniel 2:39). That kingdom was to be Medo-Persia. Persia, and the other kingdoms which were to follow, were in Daniel's future. His interpretation of the image in the king's dream was prophetic; he was giving Nebuchadnezzar what the king had desired, a view of the future. With our historical hindsight we can identify the empires which were, in Daniel's day, still in the future.

The Persian kingdom, represented by the silver chest and arms, was inferior to Babylon in quality, as silver is inferior to gold. It was greater in strength, as silver is stronger than gold. The two arms of the image indicated the coalition of two nations, the Medes whom the Persians had conquered, and the Persians.

The Belly of Bronze

Daniel continued his interpretation of the image. He said to the king, *"...Then another, a third kingdom of bronze...shall rule over all the earth"* (Daniel 2:39). This kingdom was to be the Greek Empire of Alexander the Great, which would extend from Greece to India. Alexander defeated a huge Persian army in 331 B.C., and

Persia became part of Alexander's Greek Empire. As bronze is less valuable than silver, so was the Greek kingdom inferior to the Persian kingdom. The Greek Empire was stronger than the Persian Empire as bronze is stronger than silver.

The Legs of Iron

Daniel continued the interpretation. *"And the fourth kingdom shall be as strong as iron, inasmuch as iron breaks in pieces and shatters all things; and like iron that crushes, that kingdom will break in pieces and crush all the others"* (Daniel 2:40). That strong kingdom was to be the Roman Empire which militarily crushed all the others and ruled with an iron hand. Culturally the Romans were inferior to the Greeks, as iron is less valuable than bronze. As a military force Rome was stronger than bronze.

The Roman Empire extended from Britain and Spain in the west to the Persian Gulf in the east, and from Germanic lands in the north to Egypt in the south. It encompassed every country that touched the Mediterranean Sea. It was to be the largest and the strongest of the empires of Nebuchadnezzar's dream.

The two legs of the iron portion of the image represented the division of the Roman Empire into western and eastern parts. The Emperor Diocletian in A.D. 286 split the empire to make it easier to rule and defend. Diocletian had his throne in Byzantium in the east, and he appointed Maximian as emperor of Rome in the west.

The Feet of Iron and Clay

Then Daniel interpreted the meaning of the toes of the image. The toes represented a time which is still in our future. Daniel said, *"Whereas you saw the feet and toes, partly of potter's clay and partly of iron, the kingdom shall be divided; yet the strength of the iron shall be in it, just as you saw the iron mixed with ceramic clay.*

"And as the toes of the feet were partly of iron and partly of clay, so the kingdom shall be partly strong and partly fragile.

"As you saw iron mixed with ceramic clay, they will mingle with the seed of men; but they will not adhere to one another, just as iron does not mix with clay.

"And in the days of these kings the God of heaven will set up a kingdom which shall never be destroyed; and the kingdom shall not be left to other people; it shall break into pieces and consume all these kingdoms, and it shall stand forever.

"Inasmuch as you saw that the stone was cut out of the mountain without hands, and that it broke in pieces the iron, the bronze, the clay, the silver, and the gold – the great God has made known to the king what will come to pass after this. The dream is certain, and its interpretation is sure." (Daniel 2:41-45).

King Nebuchadnezzar received Daniel's remarkable interpretation in an appropriate way. *"Then King Nebuchadnezzar fell on his face, prostrate before Daniel....The king answered Daniel, and said, 'Truly your God is the God of gods, the Lord of kings, and a revealer of secrets, since you could reveal this secret'"* (Daniel 2:46,47).

Daniel's Vision

Much later in his life under another king of Babylon,

Belshazzar, Daniel himself had a dream with visions of the kingdoms which were to come. In Daniel's dream four future kingdoms were represented by four animals. The account is told in Daniel 7. This is the first of two visions Daniel had of a series of beasts representing nations. This one occurred in the first year of the reign of Belshazzar. In the third year of Belshazzar's reign, Daniel had a similar vision of a succession of beasts which corresponded with his former vision and – like that one – also corresponded with the interpretations of the image in Nebuchadnezzar's dream. The succeeding kingdoms were always the same. It was as if the Lord was impressing on Daniel's consciousness that indeed these things were to happen to the end of the age. Daniel's second vision of beasts is given in Daniel 8.

Babylon

Again as in Nebuchardnezzar's dream Babylon is the kingdom leading the procession of empires. "*In the first year of Belshazzar king of Babylon, Daniel had a dream and visions of his head while on his bed. Then he wrote down the dream, telling the main facts.*

"Daniel spoke, saying 'I saw in my vision by night, and behold, the four winds of heaven were stirring up the Great Sea.

"'And four great beasts came up from the sea, each different from the other.

"'The first was like a lion, and had eagle's wings. I watched till its wings were plucked off; and it was lifted up from the earth and made to stand on two feet like a man, and a man's heart was given to it'" (Daniel 7:1-5).

The first three verses quoted are introductory to Daniel's vision. The sea in Scripture always refers symbolically to the mass of humanity. The Great Sea is always the Mediterranean Sea. This gives the locale of the nations which the beasts are to represent. The first beast to arise from the masses of humanity was the lion, indicating Babylon. Babylon's boundaries, like those of the following empires, extended to the shores of the Mediterranean.

The first beast was a winged lion, again showing the superiority of Babylon, the lion being the noblest of animals and the eagle being the noblest of birds. In the book of Jeremiah, Nebuchadnezzar is referred to as a lion, and his armies are called eagles. When Daniel had this vision the Babylonian Empire was coming to a close, its vassal nations already being plucked away by the Medes and Persians, as the wings were plucked from the beast. The reference to standing on two feet and being given the heart of a man may speak of Nebuchadnezzar's becoming more humane near the end of his reign.

Medo-Persia

The second beast in the vision was a bear, representing the Medo-Persian Empire. This empire was still in the future, and the vision was thereby prophetic. *"'And suddenly another beast, a second, like a bear. It was raised up on one side and had three ribs in its mouth between its teeth. And they said to it: 'Arise, devour much flesh!'"* (Daniel 7:5). Persia was stronger than Media and is the raised side of the beast. Devouring flesh refers to the empire's savagery.

In Daniel's second vision during the third year of Balshazzar's reign, Medo-Persia is described as a ram. *"In the third year of the reign of King Belshazzar a vision appeared to me – to me, Daniel – after the one that appeared to me the first time....I lifted my eyes and saw, and there, standing beside the river, was a ram which had two horns, and the two horns were high; but one was higher than the other, and the higher one came up last.*

"I saw the ram pushing westward, northward, and southward, so that no beast could withstand him; nor was there any that could deliver from his hand, but he did according to his will and became great" (Daniel 8:1,3,4).

Again the two horns of the ram indicated the consolidation of the two nations, the Medes and the Persians, with the Persians coming on the world scene after the Medes, but surpassing them in power. The ram was regarded in Daniel's day as a symbol of strength and dominance because of its butting propensity. The symbolic butting ram charged north to the Aral Sea (now part of the Soviet Union), south to the Gulf of Oman, east to northeastern India (now Pakistan), and westward to Libya and Macedonia.

Daniel lived to see the fall of Babylon to the Persians, and he was well regarded by the conquerors, keeping his position as court advisor. It was King Cyrus of the Persians who permitted the Hebrews to return from their captivity to Judea their homeland. Daniel, however, lived out his life in Babylon.

Greece

Daniel described the third beast of his first vision, a

Greek Ruins at Corinth

Corinth, a city on the Corinthian Isthmus, was a commercial power in the Greek and Roman Empires. It was also an example of the wars and bloodshed among the Greek city-states during the Age of Aries. Corinth and Sparta fought against Athens. It was Greek versus Greek with battering rams and flame throwers.

The Acropolis of Corinth, in the background of the photograph above, was excavated beginning in 1896, revealing magnificent temples. The market place, with fountains, is below the citadel. Bathrooms with facilities for running water have been uncovered.

The Corinthians were sea-going people, sailing ships using 170 rowers with oars 14 feet long. They used metal tipped rams in naval battles designed to pierce enemy ships in order to sink them.

swift leopard representing Greece two hundred years in Daniel's future. *"After this I looked, and there was another, like a leopard, which had on its back four wings of a bird. The beast also had four heads, and dominion was given to it"* (Daniel 7:6).

Alexander the Great quickly overran the Mediterranean and Middle Eastern worlds, conquering them in eleven years. He made Babylon his capital, married a Persian princess, and died in Babylon while intending to go into India. The four wings in the vision represent his four swiftly moving generals, and the four heads indicate the same generals who divided his kingdom at his death, each of the four ruling a part of it.

In the second vision Greece was depicted as a male goat, the buck which dominated the herd. *"...Suddenly a male goat came from the west, across the surface of the whole earth without touching the ground; and the goat had a notable horn between his eyes.*

"Then he came to the ram that had two horns...and ran at him with furious power.

"And I saw him confronting the ram; he was moved with rage against him, attacked the ram, and broke his two horns. There was no power in the ram to withstand him, but he cast him down to the ground and trampled him; and there was no one that could deliver the ram from his hand.

"Therefore the male goat grew very great; but when he became strong, the large horn was broken, and in place of it four notable ones came up toward the four winds of heaven" (Daniel 8:5-8).

The angel Gabriel came to Daniel to interpret the vision he had seen. Gabriel said, *"The ram which you saw, having the two horns – they are the kings of Media and Persia.*

Roman Ruins

Ruins are scattered over the territory of the Roman Empire from the Hadrian wall in Britain to the Fertile Crescent. The Roman builders built to last, mainly of stone.

In Rome the foundation of the heart of the empire remains, a monument to the might of a kingdom which the Bible predicts will be revived.

The columns in the photograph, beside a busy street in modern Rome, overlook the Roman Forum. There on seven hills a Senate made the laws of the empire. The gods and goddesses were worshiped in the temples, and orations were made by some of the world's greatest orators. Poems were read and great dramas were enacted.

There also Caesar was assassinated, emperors were betrayed, and the pride of the Age of Aries was plundered and destroyed by Germanic tribes. The iron legs of the image of Nebuchadnezzar's dream were as strong as Daniel prophesied, and as vulnerable as the law of retribution demands.

"And the male goat is the kingdom of Greece. The large horn that is between its eyes is the first king.

"As for the broken horn and the four that stood up in its place, four kingdoms shall arise out of that nation, but not with its power" (Daniel 8:20-22).

Alexander the Great was the large horn, the first king. He was reputed to have had a terrible temper which he easily lost, just as the goat raged in its fury. There is also the story that Alexander was poisoned (the horn broken) when his soldiers rebelled against going into India. The goat, the zodiacal sign of Capricorn, was the emblem of Greece. It appeared on its coins. Alexander was called the goat by his wife, and his son was called the son of the goat.

Rome

The last beast in Daniel's first vision was a dreadful monstrosity that had no name of a real animal. It represented Rome. *"After this I saw in the night visions, and behold, a fourth beast, dreadful and terrible, exceedingly strong. It had huge iron teeth; it was devouring, breaking in pieces, and trampling the residue with its feet. It was different from all the beasts that were before it, and it had ten horns"* (Daniel 7:7).

This beast in the vision, while it represents Rome, goes beyond the old Roman Empire to the revived Roman Empire at the end of the Age of Pisces. Called in prophecy the ten horns, or ten kings, or ten toes, the confederation of nations which is to come will be discussed in Chapter 5 of this book.

The two visions of Daniel left him troubled, mainly

The Sheep Pool

The photograph above was taken from the top of the old city wall of Jerusalem. The wall has a circumference of two and one half miles, encircling the Temple Mount, the busy bazaars, and the old residential section.

Adjacent to the wall is the stone sheep pool, where the animals for sacrifice were washed before bringing them to the altar in the Temple. The lambs for burnt offerings had to be without any blemish, and they had to be washed clean before being slaughtered.

The sheep pool was outside the wall, so that no defiling matter was brought within by the animal.

because he did not understand them. He was distraught by the events of the end-time among his own people. After the first vision he wrote, *"This is the end of the account. As for me, Daniel, my thoughts greatly troubled me, and my countenance changed; but I kept the matter in my heart"* (Daniel 7:28).

After the second vision he wrote, *"And I, Daniel, fainted and was sick for days; afterward I arose and went about the king's business. I was astonished by the vision, but no one understood it"* (Daniel 8:27).

It was the end-time prophecy that left Daniel bewildered. He was comforted by the angel Michael. The angel said, *"But you, Daniel, shut up the words, and seal the book until the time of the end; many shall run to and fro, and knowledge shall increase"* (Daniel 12:4). Again Michael said, *"...Go your way, Daniel, for the words are closed up and sealed till the time of the end....But you, go your way till the end; for you shall rest, and will arise to your inheritance at the end of the days"* (Daniel 12:9,13).

The Ram and the Shofar

The archaeologists who are digging up Israel's past history have been excavating around the base of the Wailing Wall. One of the interesting recent discoveries has been the uncovering of a cornerstone of the Temple which the Romans destroyed in A.D. 70. The stone, six feet wide and carved from limestone, has an inscription on it in ancient Hebrew writing. It reads: "To the house of the blowing of the Shofar..." On this spot the Temple priests blew the Shofar, a ram's horn, to notify the people of Jerusalem of the approach and end of the Sabbath.

The Parthenon

The Parthenon on the Acropolis of Athens, a white marble temple dedicated to the goddess Athena, is the best example of the classical Greek architecture of the Age of Aries. Built in the fifth century B.C., the architectural style is Doric, and the building measures 237 feet by 110 feet and is 60 feet tall. The white marble columns had iron in them to give them sheen. A forty-foot statue of Athena crafted of gold and ivory stood within.

The Parthenon was used as a Christian church beginning in A.D. 500 for almost 1000 years, then as a Moslem mosque for 200 years.

It is unknown what the interior was like precisely. In 1687 the Venetians attacked the Turks who were using the temple to store gunpowder. Ignited by a shell, the powder magazine exploded, destroying the interior of the structure.

A full-size replica of the Parthenon was built of granite in 1931 in Nashville, Tennessee. It is used as an art museum.

The ram's horn was prominent among the Israelites during the Age of Aries. Many of the religious ceremonies involved the ram and the Shofar. From the time of Mosaic Law the rites were observed. The horns of the ram were used as heralds before the Ark of the Lord. They were blown as trumpets when the walls of Jericho collapsed. The Shofar is the only ancient instrument still used in the synagogues.

The ram itself on the day of the new moon was presented as a burnt offering for the sins of the people. Under the Mosaic Law the ram was sacrificed as a peace offering. Rams' skins covered the tent of the Tabernacle in the wilderness. The psalmist sang of the ram as he praised the Lord for His goodness. *"The mountains skipped like rams, the little hills like lambs"* (Psalm 114:4).

The symbol of the ram abounded worldwide during the Age of Aries. The Egyptian deity Amon-Ra was pictured with rams' horns. The Greek goddess Palas Athene was portrayed in armor with ram's horns on her helmet. The battering rams of the Greeks, adapted from the Babylonians, had a curved ram's head at the end. The Roman soldier wore the ram on his uniform.

The Legacy of the Age of Aries

Four great civilizations during the Age of Aries prepared the way for the Age of Pisces and the Messiah which that age would usher into the world.

• Israel was planted in Canaan at the crossroads of the world where three great continents met. The exile of the Jews into Babylon cured their idolatry and their polytheistic tendencies. From then on Israel had one message: there is one God, Jehovah the Lord. Judaism's great contribution to the Arien world was monotheism.

• Two of the kingdoms in Nebuchadnezzar's dream, Babylon and Persia, were Oriental. The Oriental contribution to the world was three-fold. First was population. The masses of humanity are still in the East. They will play an important part in the events – especially the final events – of the Age of Pisces. Second was the material wealth – the lavish ostentatious courts and works of art – which has always been their cultural gift to the world. The third contribution of the Orient has been its maze of philosophies and religions – ideas that still appeal in the present contest for the human mind and allegiance.

• Riding with the Macedonian and Greek armies of Alexander the Great was the Greco-Macedonian civilization. The general and his troops thundered across Europe, Africa, and Asia, alternating pillage and appeasement, while also spreading Greek ideas and the Greek language. Soon all the world understood Greek. The beauty, exactness, and completeness of that language has never been equaled. It brought a link of common communication to the Arien world.

• The Romans, with iron armies and ruthless rule, brought law and order wherever they went. Their roads, bridges, and unified laws paved a way of contact and travel for the Piscean apostles with a missionary message.

So the Age of Aries ended, in power and expectation.

Chapter 4

The Age of Pisces

The Age of Pisces in the terms of astronomy is the period of time when the point of the spring equinox – where the equator and the ecliptic intersect – recedes slowly against the backdrop of the constellation Pisces. The constellation to the ancients made a picture of two fish swimming in opposite directions.

There are certain words that describe the astrological sign Pisces. The same words describe the Age of Pisces, which dates from the time of Christ to about A.D. 2000.

sympathy	sacrifice	illusion
seclusion	institutions	restriction
musical	spirituality	artistry

Pisces is a water sign ruled by Neptune, and its symbol is the two fish. These elements, too, figure in the Age of Pisces. The two fish are pictured in one of the stained glass windows by Marc Chagall in the synagogue of the Hadassah-Hebrew University Medical Center in Jerusalem. The two fish swimming in opposite directions appear in the window which represents the ancient tribe of Zebulum. The sign of the fish, adopted by the earliest believers, continues today as a Christian symbol.

As with the other astrological ages, the present Age of Pisces may be interpreted by observing current trends, correlating them with the characteristics of the sign Pisces and with the astrological traits of the planet Neptune.

Neptune with the Trident

This statue of Neptune, the Roman god of the sea, stands on a rock in the James River in Virginia. His counterpart was the Greek god, Poseidon. In Greek and Roman mythology the trident which he holds was used to start and stop storms and create earthquakes.

The planet Neptune, since its discovery – or rediscovery– in 1845 by an English astronomer, John C. Adams, has been the planet which astrologers associate with the sign Pisces and also with the Age of Pisces.

Astrology is older than the Greek and Roman myths. Most astrologers believe that the ancients knew about Neptune, and that the myths were based on the known effects of the planet's energies upon the earth and living things. Thus, astrology was not based on the myths, but the myths were based on astrology.

The Messianic Age Prophesied

The former age, the Age of Aries, not only prepared the way for the Age of Pisces, but it also predicted the time of the arrival of the coming age. The Bible often gives the exact timing for certain events, and this is an example of that precision.

The prophet Daniel knew precisely when the exile in Babylon would end. The scroll of Jeremiah told that the exile would last 70 years. Daniel read the Scriptures which the captives had carried to Babylon with them, so he knew when the time for their return was near.

Daniel prayed for his fellow captives, that God would forgive their collective sins, and that they would have a safe return to Judea. God not only answered his prayer affirmatively, but He also gave Daniel more. Daniel was given the precise time for the coming of the new age of the Messiah. A person living near the time of Christ, who studied the book of Daniel as Daniel had searched the writings of Jeremiah, that person would have known that the time for the coming of the Messiah was very near.

God revealed to Daniel that the span of time from the return of the captives from exile until the cutting off, that is, the crucifixion of the Messiah would be 483 years. The prophecy was specific, and history has confirmed it's fulfillment. From the time when King Artaxerxes of Persia gave permission to Nehemiah to return to Judah with a company of the captives, to inhabit the city of Jerusalem and rebuild the Temple – from that time to the crucifixion of Jesus Christ was 483 years.

The people living near the time of Christ may or may not have known the exact date of Artaxerxes' permission to Nehemiah. They most probably would not have

The Colosseum

The Colosseum, or Flavian Amphitheater, was the largest outdoor theater of ancient Rome. Its ruins now stand in downtown Rome, a monument to the early Age of Pisces, not far removed from the ferocity of the Age of Aries.

From AD 80 to AD 404 it was the site of combats between gladiators, fights between men and wild beasts, and other public entertainment – including naval battles. The arena could seat 50,000 people. The Emperor had his own entrance and his own box seat shown in the upper center of the photograph.

Stones from the edifice were later used to build medieval palaces and Christian churches. The ruins that remain are four stories tall on the intact side of the structure.

The Colosseum stands today as evidence of the deluded and cruel aspect of the Age of Pisces, an aspect which has continued in religious persecutions and religious wars throughout the age.

foreseen the date of Jesus' crucifixion. But if they had searched the Scriptures, they would have known that the time was near for the coming of the Messiah. They could have read the signs of the times.

There were groups of people and individuals who were ready for the coming of the messianic age. Anna and Simeon were two old persons who daily went to the Temple to await the Messiah. The shepherds in the fields near Bethlehem were ready for his coming. They eagerly heard and believed the angels' message that the Savior had come. Another group awaiting the Messiah were the astrologers from the east, who possessed the astrological predictions that a Deliverer was to arrive, and who set out for Jerusalem when the heavens told them that the time had come.

These people represent the three threads of the theme of this book. Anna and Simeon, praising God in the Temple expectantly, represent Bible prophecy. The shepherds, toilers of the common folk, represent anthropology, the study of mankind. The Magi, with their knowledge of the heavens, represent astrology. The thesis of this book is that three disciplines of learning – Bible prophecy, anthropology, and astrology – help explain each other. Again, as all scholars know, the particulars of knowledge mesh into the whole.

The Duality of Pisces

The Roman Empire straddled two ages. It came to power by overcoming the Greeks near the end of the Age of Aries, and its dominance extended well into the Age of Pisces. Daniel's interpretation in the former age of the

Astrologers from the East

The Wise Men or Magi, who came from the east seeking the newborn King of the Jews, were astrologers. *"After His birth astrologers from the east arrived in Jerusalem, asking, 'Where is the child who is born to be King of the Jews? We observed the rising of His star, and we have come to pay him homage'"* (Matthew 2:2). As they neared the town of Bethlehem they passed the tomb of Rachel who died giving birth to Benjamin – the tribe, Jewish astrologers believed, that was associated with the sign Pisces.

Over the stable cave where Jesus is thought to have been born stands the Church of the Nativity. In the seventh century, the story goes, the soldiers of Chosroes of Persia destroyed the other churches of the Holy Land, but spared this one when they saw its mosaics of the Wise Men in Persian dress.

he image in Nebuchadnezzar's dream ivision of the Roman Empire. The split A.D. 286 during the Age of Pisces. The Emperor iocletian became ruler of the eastern half of the enpire and resided in Byzantium, later Constantinople. Emperor Maximian ruled the western part of the empire from Rome. This division was typical of the duality of the sign Pisces. The sign's double symbol, the two fishes swimming in opposite directions, is also expressive of the sign's duality.

The divisiveness has continued throughout the age. The Roman Catholic Church, the dominant spiritual force of the Middle Ages, about A.D. 1000 separated into the western Roman Catholic Church and the Eastern Orthodox Church. A few hundred years later the Great Schism in the Roman Church was caused by dual papacies. During the Reformation, Protestant churches pulled out of the Catholic Church.

Other important divisions occurred. Astronomy split from its mother science astrology – although astrology has never left astronomy. Within astrology itself two schools have developed, the Sidereal school based on the circle of the constellations, and the Tropical school based on the zodiac of the ecliptic. The two make mutual room for each other for the most part by assigning the astrological ages to the Sidereal constellations, and the natal and mundane horoscopes to the Tropical zodiac of the ecliptic.

The symbol of Pisces also represents the dual nature of the Christian, the spiritual and the carnal, aptly described by the apostle Paul as a tug of war, with the two natures pulling in opposite directions. The constellation Pisces

Cologne Cathedral, Germany

This cathedral is one of the great basilicas of Europe built during the artistic Age of Pisces. Typical of the magnificent churches of the age, it took decades to build. Its gracefully ornate spire points to heaven to the glory of God.

The only public building of Cologne spared during the bombings of World War II, it now sits among the structures of the rebuilt city, the very old among the new.

The Cathedral is a Roman Catholic church, but is owned by the city of Cologne. The people take great pride in their locally owned church, which houses the supposed relics of the astrologers who visited Bethlehem to worship the King and give Him gifts.

like the sign is multiple. The part of the star group called the band or the bridle, which binds the two fish together, represents the limitation or restriction (another sphere of Pisces) which the Christian's dual nature imposes.

Prophecies About the Messiah

The most succinct statement that can be made about the Age of Pisces is that it has been the era of the Christian faith. Pisces is the sign of spirituality and institutions. Spanning the Christian era, the Age of Pisces has been significantly the time of the development of churches, schools, orphanages, and hospitals. These have grown primarily from a Christian concern for humanity. For almost 2000 years the institutional church has been a prime influence in the affairs of people. The universal church of believers has been a wellspring of spirituality both in and out of the organized church. In its spirituality, sympathy, and charity, the Age of Pisces has been uniquely different from all other ages.

The Age of Aries furnished the look forward to the age. The prophets of the Age of Aries made scores of prophecies about the coming Messiah, which were fulfilled in Jesus Christ at the beginning of the Age of Pisces. Some of them follow.

The Messiah will be a descendant of Abraham.

> *"God said to Abraham, 'I will bless those who bless you, and I will curse him who curses you. And in you all the families of the earth shall be blessed'"* (Genesis 12:3).

> *"The book of the genealogy of Jesus Christ, the*

Son of David, the Son of Abraham" (Matthew 1:1).

He will be from the tribe of Judah.

"The scepter shall not depart from Judah, nor a lawgiver...until Shiloh comes; and to Him shall be the obedience of the people" (Genesis 49:10).

"...The son of Amminadah, the son of Ram, the son of Perez, the son of Judah" (Luke 3:33).

He will be heir to the throne of David.

"Of the increase of His government and peace there will be no end, upon the throne of David and over His kingdom" (Isaiah 9:7).

"...The Lord God will give Him the throne of his father David...and of His kingdom there will be no end" (Luke 1:32,33).

He will be born in Bethlehem.

"But you, Bethlehem, though you are little among the thousands of Judah, yet out of you shall come the One to be ruler in Israel" (Micah 5:2).

"Joseph went up from Galilee, out of the city of Nazareth, into Judea, to the city of David, which is called Bethlehem, because he was of the house and lineage of David, to be registered with Mary his betrothed wife, who was with child...And she brought forth her firstborn Son..." (Luke 2:4,5,7).

He will come out of Egypt.

Fishing Boats on the Sea of Galilee

This lake in Galilee, seven miles wide and twelve miles long, is nestled below the hills and plains at 680 feet below sea level. Fishermen still cast their nets in this place where Jesus called his disciples to be fishers of men. The blue waters, like the fishermen, symbolize the Age of Pisces, an astrological water sign. Nazareth, Jesus' boyhood home, was nearby.

The Sea of Galilee is shaped like a harp and is sometimes called Lake Kinnereth, the Hebrew word for harp. In Jesus' day the hills were covered with trees and there was abundant vegetation. Around the lake were ten populous cities.

Today the hills are barren, except for an occasional communal kibbutz, awaiting the day when they will blossom again after the Age of Pisces has run its course.

> *"When Israel was a child, I loved him, and out of Egypt I called My Son"* (Hosea 11:1).

> *"...He took the young Child and His mother by night and departed for Egypt, and was there until the death of Herod, that it might be fulfilled which was spoken by the Lord through the prophet, saying, 'Out of Egypt I called My Son'"* (Matthew 2:14,15).

The Messiah will bind up the brokenhearted.

> *"The Spirit of the Lord is upon Me, because the Lord has annointed Me to preach good tidings to the poor; He has sent me to heal the brokenhearted..."* (Isaiah 61:1).

> Jesus quoted, *"The Spirit of the Lord is upon Me, because He has annointed Me to preach the gospel to the poor. He has sent Me to heal the brokenhearted"* (Luke 4:18).

He will be rejected by His own people.

> *"He is despised and rejected by men, a man of sorrows and acquainted with grief...He was despised, and we did not esteem Him"* (Isaiah 53:3).

> *"He came to His own, and His own did not receive Him"* (John 1:11).

He will make a triumphal entry into Jerusalem, riding on a donkey.

> *"Rejoice greatly, O daughter of Zion! Shout, O*

daughter of Jerusalem! Behold your King is coming to you; He is just and having salvation, lowly and riding on a donkey, a colt, the foal of a donkey" (Zechariah 9:9).

> *"Then they brought the colt to Jesus and threw their garments on it, and He sat on it...Then those who went before and those who followed cried out, saying: 'Hosannah! Blessed is He who comes in the name of the Lord!'... And Jesus went into Jerusalem and into the temple"* (Mark 11:7,9,11).

He will be betrayed by a close friend.

"Even my own familiar friend in whom I trusted, who ate my bread, has lifted up his heel against me" (Psalm 41:9).

> *"...Behold a multitude; and he who was called Judas, one of the twelve, went before them and drew near to Jesus to kiss Him. But Jesus said to him, 'Judas, are you betraying the Son of Man with a kiss?'"* (Luke 22:47,48).

He will be crucified with criminals.

"...He poured out His soul unto death, and He was numbered with the transgressors, and He bore the sins of many, and made intercession for the transgressors" (Isaiah 53:12).

> *"With Him they also crucified two robbers, one on His right and the other on His left.*

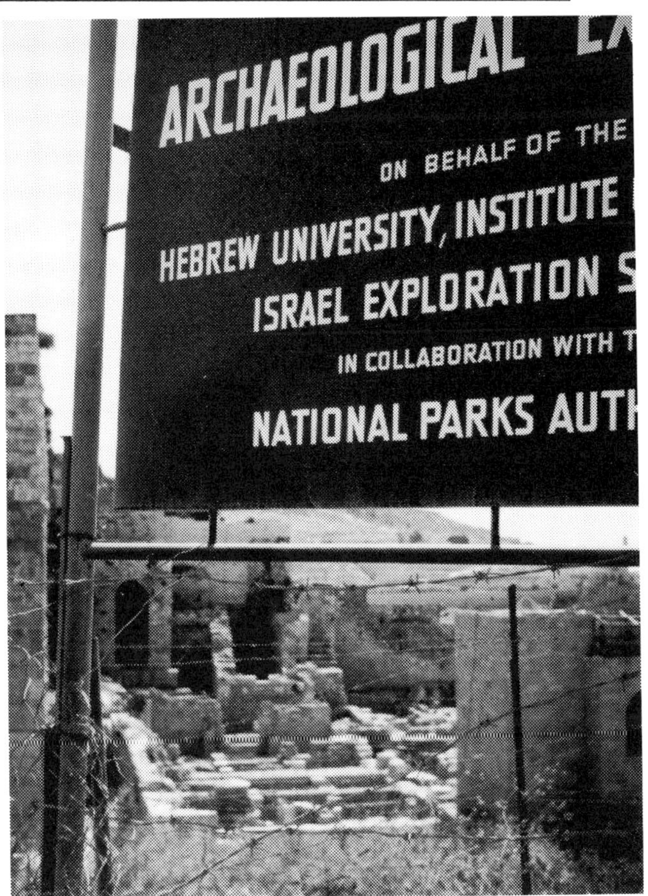

Archaeological Excavation in Jerusalem

The state of Israel, established by the United Nations on May 14, 1948, is influenced by Taurus, an earth sign. The association is seen in Israel's tenacious hold on the land. The country is a veritable archaeological museum. There has been international cooperation among many archaeological societies in respect to the digs of historical and biblical sites.

The excavation at the base of the Temple Mount in Jerusalem, shown above, has uncovered the original steps leading to the temple area on the southern side. The excavating beneath the Temple Mount, which is owned by the Moslems, requires delicate negotiations between Arab and Jewish officials for further digging. By Israel's own laws, the Jews can not encroach on property owned by any religious group.

So the Scripture was fulfilled which says, 'And He was numbered with the transgressors'" (Mark 15:27,28).

The soldiers will gamble for His clothing.

"...They look and stare at Me. They divide My garments, casting lots" (Psalm 22:17,18).

"Then they crucified Him, and divided His garments, casting lots, that it might be fulfilled which was spoken by the prophet: 'They divided My garments among them, and for My clothing they cast lots'..." (Matthew 27:35,36).

He will be buried with the rich.

"And they made His grave with the wicked – but with the rich at His death, because He had done no violence, nor was any deceit in His mouth" (Isaiah 51:9).

"Now when evening had come, there came a rich man from Arimathea, named Joseph, who himself had also become a disciple of Jesus. This man went to Pilate and asked for the body of Jesus. Then Pilate commanded that the body be given to him. And when Joseph had taken the body, he wrapped it in a clean linen cloth, and laid it in his new tomb which he had hewn out of the rock; and he rolled a large stone against the door of the tomb, and departed" (Matthew 27:57-60).

The Messiah will be resurrected.

"For You will not leave my soul in Sheol, nor will You allow Your Holy One to see corruption" (Psalm 16:10). "But God will redeem my soul from the power of the grave, for He shall receive me. Selah" (Psalm 49:15).

> *"But the angel said to them, 'Do not be alarmed. You seek Jesus of Nazareth, who was crucified. He is risen! See the place where they laid Him. But go and tell His disciples...'"* (Mark 16:6,7).

The Messiah will ascend into heaven.

"You have ascended on high..." (Psalm 68:18).

> *"So then after the Lord had spoken to them, He was received up into heaven, and sat down at the right hand of God"* (Mark 16:19).

The Sign of the Fish

The sign of the fish permeated the early Age of Pisces. The Latin word for fish was Pisces. The acronym of Jesus' initials was read as ICHTHUS, the Greek word that means fish. The spelling of the word for fish are the first letters of the name and affirmation:

Jesus Christ, Son of God, Savior.

I	=	Jesus
CH	=	CHristos (Christ)
TH	=	THeos (God)
U	=	Ulos (Son)
S	=	Soter (Savior)

Entrance to the Catacombs

This maze of catacombs, which are connecting corridors dug underground in the soft rock, is on the outskirts of Rome. Used in the first centuries by Christians as burial places, and during persecutions as meeting and hiding places, the catacomb walls have frescoes picturing religious themes and the ubiquitous sign of the fish. The tombs are cut into the walls and still hold visible human remains.

The catacombs were forgotten after Christianity became the official religion of the Roman Empire in the fourth century. They were rediscovered in AD 1578 and are now a popular tourist attraction.

The statue of the head of the saint shown above was added by the monastic order which controls the site. The monastic orders of the present era typify the seclusion and restriction which are another characteristic of Pisces.

Jesus spent much of His life on and around the beautiful Sea of Galilee. He called fishermen to be His followers and asked them to be fishers of men. By these, and by other believers who were to follow, the symbol of the fish was drawn in the sands of the seashore and charred on Roman walls. It was carved on the walls of the dark stone corridors of the catacombs where many Christians worshipped in hiding. For almost 2000 years men and women have fished for others, wooing them to the Christian faith.

Pisces rules the feet. "*...How beautiful upon the mountains are the feet of them who bring good news, who proclaim peace...who say, 'Your God reigns!'*" (Isaiah 52:7). Neptune, the ruler of Pisces, represents spiritual love and higher art. The poetic aptitude of Neptune is evident in the lofty hymns of the Christian church. Pisces rules the psychic faculties; the Piscean says, "I believe." This has been the theme of the age.

The sign of the fish appeared in profusion among the medieval basilicas of Europe during the Piscean age. The image of the two fish adorn the stained glass window in the south wall of the Chartres Cathedral in France. In the thirteenth century Baptistry of Parma, Italy, is a pair of fish sculpted by the renowned artist Antelami. The fish were often used as decorations on the facades of churches in England, as on the south door of the twelfth century Kilpeck church in Worcester. The link between Christ and the Piscean fish has been evident during the entire age, extending to the symbols and charms of today.

Fish and Loaves Mosaic

El Tabgha, sometimes called Seven Springs, is a site with gushing waters and verdant vegetation, near the Sea of Galilee. Archaeologists in 1932 uncovered this mosaic in the floor of an excavated remnant of a fourth century church. The loaves and fish commemorate the feeding of the 5000, believed by some to have taken place nearby.

By the lake today there stands a little church built of hard, dark-colored volcanic rock. It is near a bay in the Sea of Galilee where Jesus first called the disciples Andrew, Peter, and Philip to become fishers of men.

In nearby Capernaum, also by the lake, archaeologists uncovered a mosaic of the zodiac in the floor of a second century synagogue.

Art in the Age of Pisces

The Age of Pisces has been the age of artistry, illusion, and spirituality. It has given birth to new religions, most of them demanding martyrdom for the sake of one's beliefs. Wherever these religions have arisen, their beautiful monuments and structures have followed. The earth is strewn with their Neptunian imagery and splendor.

The prophet Muhammad in the A.D. 600's began the religion known today as Islam. His belief was that there was only one God, and he, Muhammad, was God's messenger. Believers in his religion are called Muslims. Most of the world's Arabs, descended from Abraham's son Ishmael, are Muslims. Islam is one of the world's largest religions today, with 650 million followers.

Islamic art is unsurpassed in beauty. The Koran, the Islamic holy book, forbids the reproduction of human and animal figures, so Muslims do not show living beings in their artistic works and structures. The Islamic houses of worship are mosques, domed buildings with towers called minarets, decorated with colored tiles in stylized designs.

Persian rugs are characteristically Islamic. Muslims have contributed to the world of art calligraphy, scroll work, paintings, pottery, and carvings. All are intricate and distinctively Islamic, including glassware, book designs, bronze and brass objects.

Astrology owes much to the Arab world. The Arabs preserved and developed astrology when some in the medieval church condemned it. The Arab aptitude in mathematics, physics, and astronomy contributed much

Dome of the Rock

The Mosque of Omar was built in the seventh century on Mount Moriah in Jerusalem. It is a sacred shrine of Islam, one of the religions rising during the Age of Pisces. Located on the Temple Mount, it occupies a site holy to both Jews and Muslims.

The splendid art of the Arabs is seen here in the golden dome and the exterior of white marble, bronze, and fine porcelain tiles. The interior is resplendent with its pillars and columns supporting the dome and roof, the stained glass windows, tapestries, and carpets from Morocco. They surround the rock of Abraham, who was ancestor of both Jew and Arab.

precision and objectivity to astrology during the middle period of the Piscean age.

The Cathedral Zodiacs

While many of the medieval churches condemned astrology as a pagan religion, all Christendom did not follow. The system was banned in some places at some times, but not universally. There were even periods when a pope would officially condemn astrology while hiring his own astrologer. The most beautiful zodiacs one can observe are in the cathedrals of Europe. These splendid works of art were put there as an integral part of the church architecture by people who viewed astrology as part of the creation of God.

In Florence, Italy, there are three impressive zodiacs in public places, two of which are in churches. In the basilica of San Miniato al Monte, a church set on a hill just outside the ancient walls of Florence, is one of the largest marble zodiacs in Europe. This zodiac was carved in A.D. 1207.

In the Baptistry of St. John in the center of the old city of Florence is a thirteenth century zodiac set in the floor. It is worn from many feet which have walked on it, but the images are still recognizable. In its center is the sun encircled by an inscription in Latin. It invites the viewer to whirl through the zodiac as does the sun each year.

A series of zodiacal images is in the fortress-like monastery of Sacra di San Michele in Italy. They are early twelfth century, possibly the oldest in Europe. The motifs of the zodiac are located vertically on the doorway, where they are intricately carved in roundels. These carvings are an example of the medieval practice of transferring symbolism of the zodiac to use in places of Christian worship. Here the constellation of the fish serves as a Christian altar.

On the facade of the cathedral of Notre Dame in Paris, France, are zodiacal signs shown in a carved relief of the thirteenth century. In this zodiac Leo the lion climbs a tree, the Scorpion has almost lost its stinger, and Cancer is represented as a crayfish. These churches were built when astrology, having been suppressed for hundreds of years, was re-entering medieval Europe. Many of the zodiacs in the cathedrals have the evidences of the additions of Arabian astrology.

The Polarity of Pisces

Opposite the constellation Pisces in the heavens is the constellation Virgo. The relationship between the two constellations is called a polarity. The Age of Pisces for the Northern Hemisphere has been for the Southern Hemisphere the Age of Virgo. From the perspective of the people who live below the equator, the point of the spring equinox – where the equator and the ecliptic intersect – is receding through the constellation Virgo.

The stars of the constellation Virgo make a picture of a young woman, a virgin. The virgin Mary's response to the angel Gabriel, when he announced to her that she would become the mother of the Messiah, was, "...Behold the maidservant of the Lord!..." (Luke 1:38). The Virgin Mary has been prominent in the religion of the Southern Hemisphere. Servanthood has been prominent in its economic condition. Both the virgin and the servant are typical of Virgo.

Today the people below the equator flex their yearnings for self-rule. This is typical of Leo, which will be the next astrological age for them, when the Northern Hemisphere enters the Age of Aquarius.

Considering the progression of the ages of the Northern and Southern Hemispheres combined, by the end of the Piscean age, the human race in one hemisphere or the other will have come full circle through the six ages of the twelve constellations. It is a phenomenon of completion. Something is new on the horizon.

Chapter 5

The End of the Age

Jesus and His disciples sat on the beautiful Mount of Olives overlooking Jerusalem. The disciples had the same questions 2000 years ago that people have today.

"When will the end come?"

"What will be the signs of the end of the age?"

"When will oppression end?"

"When will Jesus set up His kingdom?"

Notice that the questions are not about the end of the world, but are about the end of the age.

The Olivet Discourse

Jesus was patient with the questioning disciples. Not once did He say they shouldn't wonder about these things. Not once did He say they shouldn't ask the questions. And never did He refuse to answer them.

They could look down the mount across the Garden of Gethsemane on its slopes. They could see the Brook Kidron which flowed through the lowest part of the valley at the foot of the mountain. Their view continued up the next rise to the walls of Jerusalem and to the gold and marble Temple beyond. And while looking, what dire things they heard Jesus say about the area.

Their questions had been, "*...Tell us, when will these things be? And what will be the sign of Your coming, and of the end of the age?*" (Matthew 24:3).

"And Jesus answered and said to them: 'Take heed that no one deceives you. For many will come in My name, saying, 'I am the Christ,' and will deceive many. And you will hear of wars and rumors of wars. See that you are not troubled; for all these things must come to pass, but the end is not yet.

"'For nation will rise against nation, and kingdom against kingdom. And there will be famines, pestilences, and earthquakes in various places.

"'All these are the beginning of sorrows'" (Matthew 24:4-8).

Jesus said that these things were only the beginning of sorrows, because they were to be followed by things much worse. Of that coming terrible time, which will last for a period of seven years, the prophet Jeremiah had written, *"Alas! For that day is great, so that none is like it..."* (Jeremiah 30:7). The prophet Daniel had written, *"...And there shall be a time of trouble, such as never was since there was a nation, even to that time..."* (Daniel 12:1).

Now on the hillside of the Mount of Olives, Jesus was also saying to his disciples, *"For then there will be great tribulation, such as has not been since the beginning of the world until this time, no, nor ever shall be. See, I have told you beforehand"* (Matthew 24:21,25).

The Translation of the Church

Jesus will not permit His bride, the church, to go through that terrible time on earth. Her place will be in heaven with Him.

In the ancient Jewish marriage, when the girl was betrothed to her future husband, she waited for him to prepare a home for her. The home was not considered

Bethany on the Mount of Olives

On the eastern slope of the Mount of Olives lies the little town of Bethany. It was the home of Jesus' friends – Mary, Martha, and Lazarus. This was the place where Jesus called the dead Lazarus from the tomb. Today the tourist is taken down the steep, dark steps to the tomb hewn of stone, where Lazarus is supposed to have lain. As one guide says of the tomb, "If it wasn't this one, it was one like it."

It was to Bethany that Jesus led the group of apostles and believers to witness His ascension. *"And He led them out as far as Bethany, and He lifted up His hands and blessed them. Now it came to pass, while He blessed them, that He was parted from them and carried up into heaven. And they worshiped Him and returned to Jerusalem with great joy"* (Luke 24:50-52).

He left His followers to launch the Christian era of the Age of Pisces. To the same Mount of Olives He will return to end the Age of Pisces.

finished until the bridegroom's father declared it so, and approved the workmanship. Thus the timing for the wedding was in the hands of the bridegroom's father.

So it is with Jesus and the church. The night before His death He promised His disciples, who were representative of the church, His betrothed, *"In My Father's house are many mansions...I go to prepare a place for you. And if I go to prepare a place for you, I will come again and receive you to Myself; that where I am, there you may be also"* (John 14:2,3). This is the Bridegroom's promise.

The promise is repeated in the book of Revelation with an emphasis on the bride's safety, *"...I have loved you. Because you have kept My command to persevere, I also will keep you from the hour of trial which shall come upon the whole world, to test those who dwell on the earth"* (Revelation 3:9,10)

In the ancient Jewish marriage, when the bridegroom came for his bride, he took her to the home he had made for her, and the pair remained there for seven days. When Jesus comes for His bride, He will snatch her away to heaven to be with her for seven years, the period of tribulation on the earth.

The snatching away by the Bridegroom is described by the apostle Paul in 1 Thessalonians. As of today, it will involve the disappearance of 500 million Christians. *"But I do not want you to be ignorant, brethren, concerning those who have fallen asleep, lest you sorrow as others who have no hope.*

"For if we believe that Jesus died and rose again, even so God will bring with Him those who sleep in Jesus.

"For this we say to you by the word of the Lord, that we who are alive and remain until the coming of the Lord will by no

means precede those who are asleep.

"For the Lord Himself will descend from heaven with a shout, with the voice of an archangel, and with the trumpet of God. And the dead in Christ will rise first.

"Then we who are alive and remain shall be caught up together with them in the clouds to meet the Lord in the air. And thus we shall always be with the Lord.

"Therefore comfort one another with these words" (1 Thessalonians 4:13-18).

The prophet Isaiah expressed the departure beautifully. First will come the resurrection.

> *"Your dead shall live;*
> *Together with my dead body they shall arise.*
> *Awake and sing, you who dwell in dust;*
> *For your dew is like the dew of herbs,*
> *And the earth shall cast out the dead."*

Then the bride will enter heaven.

> *"Come, my people, enter your chambers,*
> *And shut your door behind you;*
> *Hide yourself, as it were, for a little moment,*
> *Until the indignation is past."*

She has left the earth and its troubles.

> *"For behold, the Lord comes out of His place*
> *to punish the inhabitants of the earth for*
> *their iniquity;*
> *The earth will uncover her blood-stains,*
> *And will no more hide her slain"*

(Isaiah 26:19-21).

Petra

Petra is the rose-red city where hundreds of homes, temples, and tombs are carved into the rock cliffs of the towering mountains. The valley surrounded by impenetrable peaks is accessible by a single mile-long path between cliffs reaching 300 feet high. In earlier times only a person on foot or horseback could make it through this entrance, but now the way has been widened to accomodate a jeep.

The narrow road – called the Siq – will welcome God's people during the Great Tribulation as a hiding place. Then the Siq will be closed by an earthquake. God's chosen ones, the Jews, will dwell in safety in the rooms carved into the mountains, while the Antichrist wreaks his final vengeance on the rest of the world for three and one half years.

The person who will rule the earth during the tribulation will be the Antichrist. But he can not appear until the church has been removed. As long as the body of Christians remains in the world as a restraining force, full-blown evil will not be able to operate. Specifically, it is the Spirit of God within the believers who does the restraining.

The people of Thessalonica had asked the apostle Paul about the day when evil would be unleashed. They had asked in particular about the coming of the Antichrist. Paul answered, *"Do you not remember that when I was still with you I told you these things?*

"And now you know what is restraining, that he may be revealed in his own time.

"For the mystery of lawlessness is already at work; only He who now restrains will do so until He is taken out of the way.

"And then the lawless one will be revealed..." (2 Thessalonians 2:5-8).

It will be at this time that the prophecies about the Antichrist in the book of Daniel will begin to unfold.

The Ten Toes in Nebuchadnezzar's Dream

The ten toes of the image in the dream of Nebuchadnezzar, king of Babylon, which are described in the book of Daniel, represent ten governments of the end time. They will arise from the old Roman Empire, which is to be revived in the last days. The Age of Pisces will end when these ten nations are in power. Their confederation will be dominated by the Antichrist.

The prophet Daniel explained the meaning of the ten toes to Nebuchadnezzar, just as he explained the rest of the image in the king's dream in Daniel 2. (See Chapter 3 of this book).

Daniel's interpretation of the image in the king's dream outlined the course of history from Daniel's time to the end time. The head of the image represented the Neo-Babylonian Empire. The chest and arms of the image stood for the next great empire, Medo-Persia. The Greek Empire of Alexander the Great followed, represented by the belly and torso of the image. The Roman Empire then arose, a divided kingdom both politically and ecclesiastically into the West and the East, represented by the two legs of the image.

Now we come to the feet and the ten toes of the image. They represent ten kingdoms which will arise from the territories of the Old Roman Empire. These kingdoms will set the end-time stage and give rise to the Antichrist.

Daniel recalled for Nebuchadnezzar what he had seen in his dream. *"This image's head was of fine gold, the chest and arms of silver, its belly and thighs of bronze, its legs of iron, its feet partly of iron and partly of clay"* (Daniel 2:32,33).

Daniel then interpreted the meaning of the feet and toes of the image. *"And as the toes of the feet were partly of iron and partly of clay, so the kingdom shall be partly strong and partly fragile. As you saw iron mixed with ceramic clay, they will mingle, but they will not adhere to one another, just as iron does not mix with clay"* (Daniel 2:42,43). The ten kingdoms will have their differences and contend with each other. The Antichrist will be the agent of cohesion among them.

Mosaic Map of Jordan

This exquisite mosaic map of Jordan, made from pieces of colored stone, graces the wall of a hotel in Amman. It shows Moab and Edom, territories which will be spared the destructive wrath of the Antichrist during the Great Tribulation. *"He shall also enter the Glorious Land, and many countries shall be overthrown: but these shall escape his hand: Edom, Moab, and the prominent people of Ammon"* (Daniel 11:41). The reason for the Antichrist's favor toward Moab and Edom is not clear.

Near the center of the map is the location of Petra, the hiding place of Revelation 12. The ancient city was occupied by the Nabataeans, a nomadic Arabian tribe, from 312 B.C. until A.D. 105, when it became part of the Roman Empire. Today it is empty except for Bedouin wanderers and the flourishing tourist trade. Petra will play its most important role in the future fulfillment of Bible prophecy.

In Daniel 7 the ten nations are called ten horns, and the Antichrist is called the little horn that will arise from them. Daniel wrote about his vision of the horns, *"I was considering the horns, and there was another horn, a little one, coming up among them....And there, in this horn, were eyes like the eyes of a man, and a mouth speaking pompous words...*

"I, Daniel, was grieved in my spirit within my body, and the visions of my head troubled me" (Daniel 7:8,15).

The Antichrist

The first thing the Antichrist will do is mesmerize the people of the world. To them he will appear as savior, with the answers to the problems of want and war. He will promise peace and abundance. And at first he will begin to deliver them.

Jesus had prophesied the world's acceptance of the Antichrist. In Jerusalem Jesus had healed a lame man on the Sabbath and thereby incurred the displeasure of the religious leaders. To them Jesus declared Himself to be the true Christ, saying, *"Most assuredly, I say to you, he who hears My word and believes in Him who sent Me has everlasting life, and shall not come into judgment, but has passed from death into life"* (John 5:24).

Then Jesus added, speaking of the Antichrist, *"I have come in My Father's name, and you do not receive Me; if another comes in his own name, him you will receive"* (John 5:43).

The Antichrist will come from a place that was both a part of Alexander the Great's Greek Empire and also a part of the old Roman Empire. The book of Daniel prophesied both as the place of origin for the coming world ruler.

The prophet Daniel wrote, "...*The people of the prince who is to come shall destroy the city and the sanctuary*" (Daniel 9:26). The people who destroyed Jerusalem and the Temple in A.D. 70 were the Romans. This verse indicates that the Antichrist will come from the ten-nation federation of the revived Roman Empire of the end time.

Daniel also specified the Greek Empire, personified as a male goat in a vision described in Daniel 8. In the following verses the large horn is Alexander the Great, who died at the peak of his military conquests. The four notable horns are the four generals who divided among themselves Alexander's empire. The little horn coming from one of them is the Antichrist.

The verses read, *"Therefore the male goat grew very great; but when he became strong, the large horn was broken, and in place of it four notable ones came up toward the four winds of heaven.*

"And out of one of them came a little horn which grew exceedingly great toward the south, toward the east, and toward the Glorious Land.

"Now it happened, when I, Daniel, had seen the vision and was seeking the meaning, that suddenly there stood before me one having the appearance of a man.

"And I heard a man's voice...who called, and said, 'Gabriel, make this man understand the vision.'

"And so he came near to where I stood, and when he came I was afraid and fell on my face; but he said to me 'Understand, son of man, that the vision refers to the time of the end.'

"And he said, 'Look, I am making known to you what shall happen in the latter time...for at the appointed time the end

shall be'" (Daniel 8:8,9,15-17).

The Greek Empire extended from Greece and Macedonia in the west to Babylon in the east. The Roman empire stretched from Britain and Spain in the west to the Middle East in the east. Where the two empires overlapped is the place from which the Antichrist comes.

Further interpretation by the angel Gabriel to Daniel, concerning the vision in Daniel 8, revealed the true nature of the Antichrist. *"And the male goat is the kingdom of Greece. The large horn...is the first king.*

"As for the broken horn and the four that stood up in its place, four kingdoms shall arise out of that nation, but not with its power.

"And in the latter time of their kingdom...a king shall arise, having fierce features, who understands sinister schemes.

"His power shall be mighty, but not by his own power; he shall destroy fearfully, and shall prosper and thrive; he shall destroy the mighty, and also the holy people.

"Through his cunning he shall cause deceit to prosper under his hand; and he shall magnify himself in his heart. He shall destroy many in their prosperity. He shall even rise against the Prince of princes; but he shall be broken without human hand" (Daniel 8:21-25).

Scenes in Heaven

Meanwhile, the scene in heaven is one of glorious reunion and praise. The Christians, who comprise the bride of Christ, have been resurrected in glorified bodies. It happened at the rapture of the church in the twinkling of an eye.

The apostle Paul wrote to the people at Corinth,

"Behold, I tell you a mystery: We shall not all sleep, but we shall all be changed – in a moment, in the twinkling of an eye, at the last trumpet. For the trumpet will sound, and the dead will be raised incorruptible, and we shall be changed....Death is swallowed up in victory" (1 Corinthians 15:51,52,54).

The apostle John wrote to the churches from the Isle of Patmos concerning what heaven is like. In contrast to the trials of his banishment to the island, he was given a vision of heaven. He was to tell what he saw in letters sent to the Christians in Asia who were suffering similar persecutions. Revelation 4 and 5 reveal what John saw.

In heaven there was One sitting on a throne. *"He who sat there was like a jasper and a sardius stone in appearance; and there was a rainbow around the throne, in appearance like an emerald.*

"Around the throne were twenty-four thrones, and on the thrones I saw twenty-four elders sitting, clothed in white robes; and they had crowns of gold on their heads.

"Before the throne there was a sea of glass, like crystal. And in the midst of the throne, and around the throne, were four living creatures..." (Revelation 4:3,4,6).

The four living creatures had aspects of the four fixed signs of the zodiac. *"The first living creature was like a lion* (Leo), *the second living creature like a calf* (Taurus), *the third living creature had a face like a man* (Aquarius), *and the fourth living creature was like a flying eagle* (Scorpio)" (Revelation 4:7). The signs in the parentheses are mine – they do not appear in the Scripture.

The four living creatures had similarities to the Assyrian winged bull and the Egyptian Sphinx of the Age of Taurus. They were similar to the vision of the four cherubim which the prophet Ezekiel saw during the Age

The Four Living Creatures

The most striking feature of the Cathedral of Cologne, Germany, is its immense size. Its stained glass windows are massive. The lower panel of one section shown above shows the four living creatures described in the book of Revelation. Astrology associates the four living creatures with the four fixed signs of the zodiac: the first living creature with the human head is Aquarius, the second creature with the head of a lion is Leo, the third creature with the head of an ox is Taurus, and the fourth creature with the head of an eagle is Scorpio.

The windows in the photograph show the living creatures with the writers of the four gospels. The living creature with the human head is paired with Luke whose gospel portrays Jesus as the Son of Man. The creature with the head of a lion is paired with Matthew who presents Jesus as the King of the Jews. The creature with the head of an ox is paired with Mark who writes of Jesus as the Servant. The fourth living creature with the head of an eagle is paired with John who presents Jesus as the Son of God.

In 1941 during World War II, an air raid shelter was built under the Cathedral. During the excavations, the foundations of an early second century church built on the same site were discovered.

of Aries. Here, in Revelation, the four living creatures chant praises to the Lord. *"And the four living creatures....do not rest day or night, saying:*

"Holy, holy, holy,
Lord God Almighty,
Who was and is and is to come!

"Whenever the living creatures give glory and honor and thanks to Him who sits on the throne, who lives forever and ever, the twenty-four elders fall down before Him who sits on the throne and worship Him who lives forever and ever, and cast their crowns before the throne, saying:

"You are worthy, O Lord,
To receive glory and honor and power;
For You created all things,
And by Your will they exist and were created"

(Revelation 4:8-11).

The Great Tribulation

For seven years after the rapture of the church, on the earth there will be a time which the Bible calls a time of trouble or the Tribulation.

Fourteen chapters of the 22 chapters in the book of Revelation describe the events of the Tribulation. These chapters, six through 19, contain much figurative language. This is the place where readers get bogged down when trying to read through the whole book.

There is an easier way to read Revelation. Regard chapter six as a summary of the entire seven years. Read

Isle of Patmos

Patmos is a small island of volcanic rock in the Aegean Sea off the coast of Asia Minor. Ten miles long and six miles wide, rocky and bare, it has volcanic hills rising 800 feet above the water level.

The Roman Emperor Domitian, brother of Titus who destroyed Jerusalem and the Temple in A.D. 70, banished the apostle John to Patmos about A.D. 95. Domitian was an absolute monarch whose cruelty made him unpopular. He executed both Jews and Christians. His wife helped to assassinate him.

John lived in a cave on the beautiful but lonely island for about 18 months. While there, the apostle received the visions from the Lord which told about the things which are and are to be hereafter. "*Write the things which you have seen, and the things which are, and the things which will take place after this*" (Revelation 1:19).

chapters one through five, then read chapter six as a summary of the Tribulation. Read chapter 19 as the climax both on the earth and in heaven. In this chapter the nations of the world meet for the Battle of Armageddon, the climax of the Great Tribulation. Also in this chapter, in heaven, the Bridegroom and the bride with their invited guests dine at the marriage supper of the Lamb, the climax of their seven-year stay in heaven. Then read chapters 20 through 22 as the end of the age and the beginning of eternity.

Four Horsemen of the Apocalypse

Now back to chapter six and the events it describes which will take place when the church – all Christian believers – leave the earth. The expression "four horsemen of the apocalypse" is used in a variety of ways, most of them having nothing to do with the real origin of the phrase. The four horsemen appear in Revelation 6, and each of them introduces a phase of the Tribulation period.

The White Horse:

The white horse represents the Antichrist.
"And I looked, and behold, a white horse. And he who sat on it had a bow; and a crown was given to him, and he went out conquering and to conquer" (Revelation 6:2).

The Red Horse:

The red horse represents war.
"And another horse, fiery red, went out. And it was

The Plain of Armageddon

This plain, also called Megiddo or Esdraelon, is the site of the world's greatest battle of the future, which is to be fought at the end of the Piscean age. More wars have been fought on this spot than any other place on earth. Napoleon Bonaparte, while viewing the plain, called it a perfect battlefield.

The vast triangular plain is bounded on the west by the Carmel Mountain range, with the Mediterranean Sea beyond. On the east are the Sea of Galilee and the Jordan River. The north by way of the highway to Damascus affords an approach from Lebanon and Syria, while the south gives entrance to Jerusalem.

Here, according to prophecy, the blood will run as high as the horses' bridles.

granted to the one who sat on it to take peace from the earth, that people should kill one another; and there was given to him a great sword"
(Revelation 6:4).

The Black Horse:
The black horse represents famine.
"...And I looked, and behold, a black horse, and he who sat on it had a pair of scales in his hand. And I heard a voice saying, 'A quart of wheat for a day's wages, and three quarts of barley for a day's wages...'"
(Revelation 6:5,6).

The Pale Horse:
The pale horse represents death.
"And I looked, and behold, a pale horse. And the name of him who sat on it was Death, and the Grave followed with him. And power was given to them over a fourth of the earth, to kill with sword, with hunger, with death, and by the beasts of the earth"
(Revelation 6:8).

The apostle John saw these things in the vision he received on the Isle of Patmos. The remaining verses in chapter six of Revelation add to the picture of horrors. *"...Behold, there was a great earthquake; and the sun became black as sackcloth of goat's hair, and the moon became like blood.*

"And the stars of heaven fell to the earth, as a fig tree drops its late figs when it is shaken by a mighty wind.

"Then the sky receded as a scroll when it is rolled up, and every mountain and island was moved out of its place.

"And the kings of the earth, the great men, the rich men, the commanders, the mighty men, every slave and every free man, hid themselves in the caves and in the rocks of the mountains, and said to the mountains and rocks, 'Fall on us and hide us...for the great day of wrath has come, and who is able to stand?'" (Revelation 6:12-17).

The Great Tribulation will end with the Battle of Armageddon. It is the Lord who will give the victory in the Battle of Armageddon. The coming of the Lord Jesus Christ will end the battle. *"From his mouth there went a sharp sword with which to smite the nations; for he it is who shall rule them with an iron rod....'King of kings and Lord of lords'"* (Revelation 19-15-16).

Concerning these times Jesus said, *"With all these things the birth-pangs of the new age begins"* (Matthew 24:8). After the last dregs of the end of the Age of Pisces, there will begin a new age on the earth. Astrology calls it the Age of Aquarius. Christians call it the Millenium.

Chapter 6

The Age of Aquarius

The Age of Aquarius will be the period of time when the point of the spring equinox – where the equator and the ecliptic intersect – will recede against the backdrop of the constellation Aquarius. To the ancients the stars of that constellation made a picture of a water-bearer.

There are words that describe the astrological sign Aquarius. The same words describe the Age of Aquarius, which will probably date from about 2000 A.D. to 3000 A.D.

friendship	goals	freedom
brotherhood	hopes	detachment
humanitarian	scientific	unpredictable

Aquarius is an air sign ruled by Uranus, and its symbol is the water-bearer. These elements, too, will figure in the Age of Aquarius.

One thousand years will be the span of the Aquarian Age, according to the Bible, the length of the reign of Jesus Christ on the earth. The duration of the Age of Aquarius, half as long as the other ages, will be due to the fact that it will take only half as long for the point of the spring equinox to recede against the constellation. Perhaps the cataclysmic events at the end of the Age of Pisces will change the wobble of the earth's axis, which determines the Precession of the Equinoxes and the length of the astrological ages.

The Coming Golden Age

Of all the ages of the history of mankind, the Age of Aquarius has been the most anticipated, the most talked about, and also the least understood. People eagerly grasp the concept of the coming Age of Aquarius. Perhaps this is because of the longing for a better era which is shared in the hearts of most people. Not only those who understand astrology and the astrological ages, but others, too, look forward to a new day characterized by brotherly love and peace on earth. The exact time of the start of the Age of Aquarius can not be precisely predicted, because the exact point of the beginning of the constellation can not be determined.

Most of humanity through the centuries have longed for a golden age. The idea appears in literature again and again – in Plato's *Republic,* in Sir Thomas More's *Utopia,* in the *City of the Sun* by the friar Campanella of Naples, and Francis Bacon's *The New Atlantis.* The quatrains of Nostradamus predicted that after many wars there would be an age of peace. These works have been poetic, romantic, or scholarly, but none of them have accelerated the coming of such an age.

That day of universal peace and brotherhood is certain to follow the final agonies of the Age of Pisces. It will dawn as an age of harmony, tolerance, peace, and justice. These are the expressions most often used to describe the Age of Aquarius. They are also the words used to describe the Christian Millennium.

Unlike the other astrological ages already discussed in this book, the Age of Aquarius can not be described with hindsight. Hindsight, of course, is handier than foresight.

It is easier to relate an event after the fact than it is to foretell it. We can uncover the previous ages with archaeology and research. We may correlate the discoveries concerning them with the characteristics of the corresponding astrological sign and the planet which ruled the age. Only the latter may also be done concerning the Age of Aquarius. The characteristics of Aquarius and Uranus give us broad hints about the age and the future. Their traits give us clues.

Words frequently used to describe the sign of Aquarius are humanitarian, independent, and innovative. They characterize the Aquarian person as they do the Aquarian age. Aquarius encourages individualistic urges. The coming age will satisfy the concern for the individual. Human rights will be extended to all people of the world. Want, tyranny, and oppression will disappear.

Aquarius is depicted as the propellant of the unexpected, the different, and the original, not fitting any previous mold. Such will be the Aquarian Age. There will be changes, always for the better. Changes may occur so rapidly as to seem erratic, as Aquarius often seems. The rapid changes, however, will be positive.

There will be a reconciliation between science and humanity. The concern for the environment will meet with international cooperation. Discovery, technology, and the human will, all working together, solve the problems of establishing world peace and eliminating poverty and hunger.

These natural tendencies of Aquarius will prevail. The impetus and the momentum of these glorious achievements, however, will be supernatural. The coming golden age will be made possible because Jesus Christ will have come again and will be reigning on the earth. The prophet Daniel 2500 years ago saw His reign in the dream of Nebuchadnezzar.

The Stone in the Dream

When King Nebuchadnezzar of Babylon demanded that someone tell him what his troubling dream had been, the prophet Daniel recalled it for him. Daniel said, *"You watched while a stone was cut out without hands, which struck the image on its feet of iron and clay, and broke them in pieces.*

"Then the iron, the clay, the bronze, the silver, and the gold were crushed together, and became like chaff from the summer threshing floors; the wind carried them away so that no trace of them was found. And the stone that struck the image became a great mountain and filled the whole earth.

"This is the dream. Now we will tell the interpretation of it before the king" (Daniel 2:34-36).

Then Daniel interpreted the meaning of the stone.

"And in the days of these kings the God of heaven will set up a kingdom which shall never be destroyed; and the kingdom shall not be left to other people; it shall break in pieces and consume all these kingdoms, and it shall stand forever.

"Inasmuch as you saw that the stone was cut out of the mountain without hands, and that it broke in pieces the iron, the bronze, the clay, the silver, and the gold – the great God has made known to the king what will come to pass after this. The dream is certain, and its interpretation is sure" (Daniel 2:44,45).

The stone in Daniel 2 brought about the kingdom of

the Messiah. His coming is described in Daniel 7.

"I was watching in the night visions,
And behold, One like the Son of Man,
Coming with the clouds of heaven!...
Then to Him was given dominion and
glory and a kingdom,
That all peoples, nations, and
languages should serve him.
His dominion is an everlasting dominion,
Which shall not pass away,
And His kingdom the one
Which shall not be destroyed"
(Daniel 7:13,14).

The Capital City

The King at His coming will touch ground on the Mount of Olives, the place from which He ascended almost 2000 years ago. He will establish Jerusalem as the capital of His government, a city which will be drastically changed by the event of His coming. As the feet of Jesus touch the Mount of Olives, the mountain will split in two from east to west. Jerusalem at once will become a port city with its waters gushing westward to the Mediterranean Sea and eastward to the Dead Sea.

"And in that day His feet will stand on
the Mount of Olives,
Which faces Jerusalem on the east.
And the Mount of Olives shall be split in two,
From east to west,

The Eastern Gate

The Eastern Gate of the walls of Jerusalem faces the Mount of Olives.

The King of the Millennial Kingdom is prophesied to enter Jerusalem through the Eastern Gate, often called the Golden Gate.

To keep this prophecy from being fulfilled, the Turks who occupied the city in the 7th century A.D. sealed the gate as pictured above. They unwittingly helped to insure the prophecy's fulfillment, for the prediction states that the eastern gate will "break open" for the King.

Both Moslem and Jewish burial grounds are in front of the eastern wall and gate. The dead are buried with their feet toward the east, so that on resurrection morning they will rise to face the east.

Making a very large valley;
Half of the mountain shall move toward
the north
And half of it toward the south....
Thus the Lord my God will come,
And all the saints with him.
And in that day it shall be
That living waters shall flow from Jerusalem,
Half of them toward the eastern sea
And half of them toward the western sea...
And the Lord shall be King over all
the earth..."

(Zechariah 14:4,5,8,9).

The prophets revealed other facts about the capital city. On the banks of the waters of Jerusalem will be a place of abundance.

"And it will come to pass in that day
That the mountains will drip with new
wine,
The hills will flow with milk,
And all the brooks of Judah shall be
Flooded with water..."

(Joel 3:18).

It will be a city of peace and prosperity.

"For thus says the Lord,
'Behold, I will extend peace to her like
a river...'"

(Isaiah 66:12).

Jerusalem will be a city of beauty.

"I will make your pinnacles of rubies,
Your gates of crystal,
And all your walls of precious stones"
(Isaiah 54:12).

Jerusalem will be a city of rejoicing.

"Rejoice with Jerusalem,
And be glad with her...
Rejoice for joy with her...
That you may feed and be satisfied...
That you may drink deeply and be
delighted
With the abundance of her glory"
(Isaiah 66:10,11).

The People of the Millennium

The events which will usher in the Age of Aquarius will be dramatic and sudden. The armies of the nations will be mustered for the Battle of Armageddon. Jesus will appear in the sky on a white horse. He will be accompanied by the Christian believers of all the centuries. *"Then I saw heaven opened, and behold, a white horse. And He who sat on him was called Faithful and True....His eyes were like a flame of fire, and on His head were many crowns...And the armies in heaven, clothed in fine linen, white and clean, followed Him on white horses"* (Revelation 19:11,12).

Those on the white horses, Christian believers, will have been in heaven for seven years since the translation of the church. They are the bride of Christ, who have partaken of the marriage supper of the Lamb. *"Let us be glad and rejoice and give Him glory, for the marriage of the Lamb has come, and His wife has made herself ready. And to her it was granted to be arrayed in fine linen, clean and bright, for the fine linen is the righteous acts of the saints...Blessed are those who are called to the marriage supper of the Lamb...These are the true sayings of God"* (Revelation 19:7-9).

These will reign with Christ on the earth for a thousand years, as co-regents. *"And I saw thrones, and they sat on them, and judgment was committed to them....And they lived and reigned with Christ for a thousand years. Blessed and holy is he who has part in the first resurrection...They shall be priests of God and of Christ, and shall reign with Him a thousand years"* (Revelation 20:4,6). The people they will rule over are the ones left on the earth in their natural bodies after the tribulations of the Age of Pisces. These people will repopulate the earth.

The prophet Daniel described the privilege which will be granted to the faithful.

"Then the kingdom and dominion,
And the greatness of the kingdoms
under the whole heaven,
Shall be given to the people,
the saints of the Most High..."
(Daniel 7:27).

The apostle Paul wrote, *"Do you not know that the saints*

Sheep and Goats at Galilee

One of the world-wide events when the King begins his reign will be the judgment of the nations. The Age of Aquarius will begin with the purge of the nations. In Matthew 25 Jesus makes it clear that the multitudes who will come against Jerusalem for the Battle of Armageddon will not enter the Kingdom of the Millennium.

There will be a division of the sheep and the goats – of the nations who have blessed Jesus' brothers, Israel, and those who have cursed Israel.

The pastoral scene above beside the Sea of Galilee shows the shepherds who tend both the goats and the sheep. The goats' black hair is used as it was in the day of Abraham to cover the Bedouins' tents. The sheep are kept for milk and skins. Goats and sheep are often kept together. In the figurative language of the nations' judgment, they will be separated.

will judge the world?" (1 Corinthians 6:2). To Timothy the young preacher he wrote, *"If we endure, we shall also reign with Him..."* (2 Timothy 2:13).

Each person's place in the millennial government will depend at least in part on what is done during one's lifetime. *"...I will reward each one of you according to his deeds....To him who is victorious I will grant a place on my throne..."* (Revelation 3:11,21).

The twelve apostles who were with Christ during His earthly ministry will have a special place in the government of the world during His millennial reign. When the impetuous Peter asked Jesus what would be their reward for following Him, Jesus replied, *"...Assuredly I say to you, that when the Son of Man sits on the throne of His glory, you who have followed Me will also sit on twelve thrones, judging the twelve tribes of Israel"* (Matthew 19:28).

Jesus repeated that the promise to His disciples on the night before His death. *"...You are those who have continued with Me in My trials. And I bestow upon you a kingdom, just as My Father bestowed one upon Me, that you may eat and drink at My table in My kingdom, and sit on thrones judging the twelve tribes of Israel"* (Luke 22:28-30).

The Earth

The Age of Aquarius will be that wondrous age when all nature will be at peace. The earth will again become a garden and bloom for a thousand years, lush and beautiful, and perpetually watered. *"For waters shall break forth in the wilderness and streams in the desert; the burning sand shall become a pool, and the thirsty ground springs of*

Grape Vines in the Desert

Lush grape vines are growing in Israel where once were only rocks and dirt. At one time in the land of Canaan it took two men to carry one cluster of grapes. *"...They cut down a branch with one cluster of grapes; they carried it between two of them on a pole..." (Numbers 13:23).*

The land will again be restored. *"...Israel shall blossom and bud, and fill the face of the world with fruit"* (Isaiah 27:6). *"The wilderness and the wasteland shall be glad...and the desert shall rejoice and blossom as the rose. It shall blossom abundantly and rejoice..."* (Isaiah 35:1,2).

The beginning of the agricultural restoration in Israel today is one of the signs of the times which Jesus said to read expectantly.

water..." (Isaiah 35:6,7).

The symbol of Aquarius is the water bearer who pours out his precious cargo on the earth to refresh it. So it will be in the Age of Aquarius. Wastelands will be irrigated and productive. Even the weather will be harnessed and turned into blessing, and abundance will be the norm. The ecology of the earth will be perfected, as environmental protection and maximum development will be a reality for human, plant, and animal life.

For the planet itself, the age will be a period of blessedness. The earth will be released from the curse of sin which it has endured for thousands of years. When sin entered the human race in the Garden of Eden, the result was that the earth was also cursed. God said to Adam, *"...Accursed shall be the ground on your account... It will grow thorns and thistles for you, none but wild plants for you to eat"* (Genesis 3:17,18).

In addition to the curse of sin, the inhabitants of the earth have added their pollution to the problems of nature. Long ago were prophesied the conditions of the earth as it is today. *"The earth itself is desecrated by the feet of those who live in it"* (Isaiah 24:5). Those words were written 2700 years ago. The same verse in the Revised Standard Version of the Bible reads, *"The earth lies polluted under its inhabitants."*

The curse is described in the New Testament with all its devastation, but also with a hint of hope for a future time. *"For the created universe waits with eager expectation... It was made the victim of frustration, not by its own choice... Yet always there was hope because the universe itself is to be freed from the shackles... Up to the present...the whole created universe groans in all its parts..."* (Romans 8:19-22).

The Lion and the Lamb

The prophet Isaiah predicted that in the Age of Aquarius,

"The wolf shall dwell with the lamb,
The leopard shall lie down with the young goat,
The calf and the young lion and the fatling together;
And a little child shall lead them.
The cow and the bear shall graze;
Their young ones shall lie down together;
And the lion shall eat straw like the ox.
The nursing child shall play by the cobra's hole,
And the weaned child shall put his hand in the viper's den.
They shall not hurt nor destroy in all My holy mountain,
And the earth shall be full of the knowledge of the Lord
As the waters cover the sea"
(Isaiah 11:6-9).

At a future date all nature, now cursed, will be restored to the conditions of the Garden of Eden. *"Before you mountains and hills shall break into cries of joy, and all the trees of the wild shall clap their hands, pine-trees shall shoot up in place of camel-thorn, myrtles instead of briars...* (Isaiah 55:12,13). *"...The pastures shall be green, the trees shall bear fruit..."* (Joel 2:22). All creation will return to its Edenic state.

It will be a time of plenty. *"Men shall build houses and live to inhabit them, plant vineyards and eat their fruit"* (Isaiah 65:21). *"The threshing floors shall be heaped with grain, the vats shall overflow with new wine and oil... And you shall eat, you shall eat your fill and praise the name of the Lord your God who has done wonders for you"* (Joel 2:24,26).

The Government

The apostles and the faithful of the Lord will be the officials of a government headed by Jesus Christ the King. *"...The government will be upon his shoulder, and his name will be called 'Wonderful, Counselor, Mighty God, Everlasting Father, Prince of Peace.' Of the increase of his government and of peace there will be no end, upon the throne of David, and over his kingdom, to establish it, and to uphold it with justice and with righteousness..."* (Isaiah 9:6,7).

It will be a government of justice for all the people of the earth. Jesus came into this world in human form, in this writer's opinion, as an Aquarian, under the humanitarian sign of justice. How fitting was the human heritage of the One who was to rule the Aquarian age.

During the Age of Aquarius all men and women will be brothers and sisters. The justice of the government

Children on the Mediterranean Coast

Children play on the shore of the Mediterranean Sea near Joppa, where Jonah set sail for Tarshish. *"Children are a heritage from the Lord..."* (Psalm 127:3).

The Millennial age will insure the safety and well-being of children. *"The streets of the city shall be full of boys and girls playing in the streets"* (Zechariah 8:5). *"All your children shall be taught by the Lord, and great shall be the peace of your children"* (Isaiah 54:13).

will be reflected in the lifestyle of the people. *"Behold a king shall reign with righteousness and his rulers rule with justice.... He shall judge the poor with justice and defend the humble in the land with equity..."* (Isaiah 32:1;11:4). It will be an era of security and safety. *"Once again shall old men and old women sit in the streets...and the city shall be full of boys and girls, playing in the streets"* (Zechariah 8:4,5).

There will be security with peace throughout the world *"...They shall beat their swords into mattocks and their spears into pruning-knives; nation shall not lift sword against nation nor ever again be trained for war, and each man shall dwell under his own vine, under his own fig-tree, undisturbed..."* (Micah 4:3,4).

Today's increasingly sophisticated technology points to the Aquarian age, when material assets will be used for universal benefit. Electricity, electronics, electromagnetic energy, jet propulsion, and nuclear energy have been put to use only recently in human history, an indication of the nearness of the coming age, when cosmic energies will be bridled, controlled, and released for the good of humanity.

Wisdom shall prevail both in government and among the people. Individualism and personal freedom will not infringe on the well-being of others. Decisions will be based on a *"spirit of wisdom and understanding, a spirit of counsel and power, a spirit of knowledge and the fear of the Lord"* (Isaiah 11:2).

Religion In The Golden Age

All the earth will worship the Lord. *"...As the waters fill the sea, so shall the land be filled with the knowledge of the*

The Scroll of Isaiah

The oldest scroll of Isaiah in existence was among the Dead Sea Scrolls found by the shepherd boys in the caves of the desert in southern Israel near the Dead Sea. The jars of scrolls were discovered near the excavations of the community of the Essenes, a reclusive group of scholars who were probably the scribes of the manuscripts. The scroll of Isaiah from about A.D. 200 is amazingly similar to the book as published in to-day's Bibles. The scroll, made from 17 pieces of parchment sewn together, is 24 feet long.

The prophet Isaiah was the author of the loftiest prophecies of the messianic age and the reborn earth.

Lord" (Isaiah 11:9). *"...On that day the Lord shall be one Lord and his name the one name"* (Zechariah 14:9).

People of all nations will come to the house of the Lord, the Temple of the Millennium which is to be rebuilt in Jerusalem. *"In days to come the mountain of the Lord's house shall be...lifted high above the hills. And it shall come to pass that everyone who is left of all the nations...shall go up from year to year to worship the King, the Lord of hosts, and to keep the Feast of Tabernacles"* (Zechariah 14:16).

"People shall come streaming to it, and many nations shall come and say, 'Come, let us climb to the house of...God....that he may teach us his ways and we may walk in his paths'" (Micah 4:1-2). There will be joy in the hearts of the people. *"For you there shall be songs, as on a night of sacred pilgrimage, your hearts glad, as the hearts of men who walk to the sound of the pipe on the way to the Lord's hills, to the rock of Israel"* (Isaiah 30:29).

The destination of these sacred pilgrimages, the Temple of Jerusalem, is described in detail in the book of the prophet Ezekiel. The imagery which decorates the Temple will include the symbols of the Age of Aquarius and its counterpart the Age of Leo. The symbol of Aquarius is a man, the water-bearer, and the symbol of Leo is the lion. They will be displayed in the carvings of the cherubim on the walls of the Temple.

"From the ground up to the windows and above the door, both in the inner and outer chambers, round all the walls, inside and out, were carved figures, cherubim and palm trees, a palm between every pair of cherubim. Each cherub had two faces: one the face of a man, looking towards one palm-tree, and the other the face of a lion, looking towards another palm tree. Such was the carving round the whole of the temple" (Ezekiel

Herod's Temple

Solomon's Temple on Mount Moriah in Jerusalem was the first to be built on that site. It was destroyed by the Babylonians under Nebuchadnezzar in 586 B.C. Herod's Temple, the second, shown here from the model in the garden of the Jerusalem Hotel, was built by the exiles under Zerubbabel returning from Babylon. It was refurbished by Herod the Great, and destroyed in A.D. 70 by the Romans.

Two more temples are predicted to be built on the same Temple Mount. The first will be during the tribulation period, and the second during the Millennium. The latter is described in the book of Ezekiel 41 through 46, a magnificent structure the length of three football fields.

41:17-19). The astrological symbols of the ages which are opposite each other and occur simultaneously in history, as Aquarius and Leo, are always shown together in biblical imagery, as the lion and the man are shown together here.

The Polarity of Aquarius

Opposite the constellation Aquarius in the heavens is Leo. The constellation Leo is seen by the people of the Southern Hemisphere, while the population of the Northern Hemisphere are viewing Aquarius. The opposing relationship between the two constellations is called a polarity. The same relationship exists between the two astrological signs Aquarius and Leo.

During the Age of Aquarius and the coinciding Age of Leo, the polarity of the two signs will blend the humanitarian qualities of Aquarius with the organizational and authoritative traits of Leo. The Age of Aquarius is the next coming age of the people of the Northern Hemisphere. For people living in the Southern Hemisphere the coming age will be the Age of Leo. The influence of Leo will be felt particularly below the equator.

For these, Jesus *"the Lion of the tribe of Judah"* (Revelation 5:5) will bring deliverance from bondage of many kinds. For them it will be an era of self-rule and blossoming ego. It will come after a long history of servitude and suppression. The present age for the Southern Hemisphere, during the northern Age of Pisces, has been the Age of Virgo, which is the sign of service.

This will be but one of the remarkable changes in the coming Age of Aquarius, which will be the Millennium prepared by the Lord and promised in His Word.

Human good intentions, hopes, and advanced technology will not be sufficient to bring about that golden age. Rather it will be the fulfillment of the dream of Artaban, the other wise man in Henry Van Dyke's story, who sought the universal Messiah. *"Your eyes will see the King in His beauty..."* (Isaiah 33:17).

Chapter 7

Progressed Sun Signs

Now make some predictions of your own about your future personal characteristics. This can be done by a method called "progressed sun signs." All you need to know is the date of your birth, which will be used with the tables at the end of this chapter.

Just as one is able to view in a broad scope the progression of the astrological ages, one age after another, so is a person able to view the development of one's own personality in its entirety. Your progressed sun sign indicates one way in which your personality develops from birth.

A Day for a Year

The progressed sun sign (or PSS) is found by counting each year of life as one day. To determine the PSS at age 30, for example, count forward 30 days from the birth date on the calendar. The sun's position on the ecliptic or the zodiac on that day is the PSS.

Consider a Taurus born on May 12. To ascertain the PSS at age 30, count forward 30 days from May 12 to June 11. For this Taurus person at age 30, the PSS is Gemini. Proceed in this way at any age, counting one day forward for each year of life, to find your progressed sun sign.

The idea of "a day for a year" is popular with most astrologers. The concept is taken from the prophetic symbolism in the Bible. It appears in the book of Ezekiel. The Lord, explaining the symbolism of a certain prophecy, said to the prophet Ezekiel, "*....I count one day for every year*" (Ezekiel 4:6 NEB).

The idea is also in the book of Daniel. In Daniel 9 the prophet wrote about a period of time in Israel's future which was to be in duration 490 years, but termed it "*seventy weeks of days*" (Daniel 9:24). A week of days is seven days. Seventy weeks of days multiply to 490 days. Daniel thus let the figurative 490 days represent 490 years. This is the same concept used in astrology when determining the position of the progressed sun.

Your Changing Personality

Your progressed sun sign shows a natural development of personality from birth. Your birth chart is a circle showing a map of the solar system at the time of your birth. The accumulated knowledge of astrology explains the effect on an individual's personality of the placements in the horoscope, or birth chart, of the sun, moon, and the planets.

As the sun moves through the chart from its natal position, one day for each year of life, its progression continues to make an imprint on your nature. Its movement of one day equals about one degree on the circle of the chart. At age one the progressed sun's position is one day after birth or one degree forward on the chart. At age ten, the progressed sun's position is ten calendar days after birth, or ten degrees forward on the chart.

As a specific example, a person born on October 4 has a birth chart, or horoscope, with the sun at 11 degrees Libra. Each sign of the zodiac consists of 30 degrees on the circle of the chart. Therefore, when the person born on October 4 with the sun at 11 degrees Libra reaches age

20, the progressed sun enters the next sign and is now at 1 degree Scorpio.

For the Libran a new phenomenon occurs. The Libran begins to assume the characteristics of Scorpio. The entrance of the progressed sun into the next sign often explains a definite change in personality which the person and others notice. While the original indications of the natal chart stay with the individual for a lifetime, life is never static. The Libran is still a Libran, but for the duration of the sun's stay in Scorpio – for about 30 years – the person also has the traits of Scorpio. The personality has become more complex, more interesting.

Personality is ever changing and developing. As the Libra native grows still older, at the age of 49, the progressed sun leaves Scorpio and enters Sagittarius. The Scorpio characteristics recede as the Libra person now adds Sagittarian characteristics to the native Libran personality.

Traditional astrology assigns the following traits to each of the twelve sun signs of the zodiac. Your date of birth determines your sun sign. The following summaries describe both your natal sun sign and your progressed sun sign.

Aries

March 21 to April 19

Aries, whose symbol is the ram, is a fire sign. People whose sun sign is Aries are ambitious, impulsive, enterprising, impatient, courageous, and hot-tempered.

They have great energy. They like a new challenge, but often do not finish what they start. They are outspoken, generous, and forgiving. They like to compete, are good athletes and competent leaders. They like to have their own way. As a cardinal sign, they initiate action.

Taurus

April 20 to May 20

Taurus, whose symbol is the bull, is a practical earth sign. People whose sign is Taurus are loyal, patient, and steadfast. They appreciate beauty, fine furnishings and clothes, and comfort. They are affectionate, kind, sensuous, determined, and stubborn. They perform tasks slowly and thoroughly. They often get their self-esteem from owning things. They usually have very pleasant voices. Unless pushed too far, they have pleasing dispositions.

Gemini

May 21 to June 20

Gemini, whose symbol is the twin brothers, is a mental air sign. People whose sun sign is Gemini are curious, restless, and talkative. They are quick learners, clever, and indecisive because they can see all sides of an issue. They have high-strung nervous systems and changeable dispositions. They are gregarious, really enjoy other people, and are good communicators. They see the green grass on the other side of the fence and are likely to go there.

Cancer

June 21 to July 22

Cancer, whose symbol is the crab, is a sensitive water sign. People whose sun sign is Cancer are imaginative, artistic, home-loving, family-oriented, and intuitive. They have changeable moods. They often cling to the past. They are aware of the public pulse and public needs. They are acquisitive and are usually successful in business. They are nurturing and make good counselors. They work well with children and are good parents.

Leo

July 23 to August 22

Leo, whose symbol is the lion, is a warm fire sign. People whose sun sign is Leo are genial, strong-willed, kind, and energetic. They are considered the royal sign. They have positive outlooks and charming personalities. At times they can appear bossy and proud. They like center stage and are good leaders. They do things with flair, style, and drama. They are loyal, romantic, creative, and generous.

Virgo

August 23 to September 22

Virgo, whose symbol is the virgin, is a practical earth sign. People whose sun sign is Virgo are tidy, careful, orderly, intelligent, and efficient. They are discriminating and pay attention to details. They tend to find fault with things which others think are unimportant. They are dependable and well-mannered. The intellectual life is important to them. They are analytical.

Libra

September 23 to October 22

Libra, whose symbol is a pair of scales, is a social air sign. People whose sun sign is Libra like things in balance and in harmony. They appreciate style and elegance. They are artistic, sociable, friendly, and pleasant. They dislike conflict and change, and they are often indecisive. They are good mediators. They like pleasing surroundings. They are romantic, in love with love. Ugliness makes them unhappy. They are at home in the arts.

Scorpio

October 23 to November 21

Scorpio, whose symbol is the scorpion or the eagle, is

an emotional water sign. People whose sun sign is Scorpio are intense, deep, secretive, resourceful, and passionate. They have magnetic personalities. They are good leaders and command respect. They are seekers of truth, good researchers and investigators. They make changes by uprooting. They are loyal and insist on fairness.

Sagittarius

November 22 to December 21

Sagittarius, whose symbol is the archer, is a spirited fire sign. People whose sun sign is Sagittarius are outgoing, outspoken, enthusiastic, and optimistic. They are restless, freedom-loving, and do not want to be told what to do. They like to explore terrain as well as ideas. They are cheerful, like change and travel, and like to expand their horizons. They have a good sense of humor.

Capricorn

December 22 to January 20

Capricorn, whose symbol is the goat, is a pragmatic earth sign. People whose sun sign is Capricorn are serious, ambitious, cautious, and dignified. They are patient, dependable, and efficient. They care what people think. They are perfectionists and may be opinionated. They are able to overcome difficulties and hardships. They are sincere and responsible.

Aquarius

January 21 to February 19

Aquarius, whose symbol is the water bearer, is an altruistic air sign. People whose sun sign is Aquarius are sociable, humanitarian, freedom-loving, independent, and intellectually curious. They champion the needy. They value friendships and are loyal friends themselves. They are fair-minded toward everyone. They are unpredictable, like change, and are ahead of their time. They are good business persons. Aquarians like to live and let live.

Pisces

February 20 to March 20

Pisces, whose symbol is the two fishes swimming in opposite directions, is an emotional water sign. People whose sun sign is Pisces are kind, sympathetic, friendly, and vague. They are mystical and poetic. They are aware of the moods and needs of others. Sometimes they lack a sense of reality. They have vivid imaginations and intuitive intelligence. They must take care not to be deceived by unscrupulous persons. They believe the best of everyone.

Sun Sign Temperaments

As your sun sign makes its first progression into another sign, the nature of your personality will also take on another type of temperament. If your natal sun sign is a spirited fire sign (Aries, Leo, or Sagittarius), your progressed sun will move into a practical earth sign (Taurus, Virgo, or Capricorn).

If your natal sun sign is a practical earth sign, your progressed sun will move into a social air sign (Gemini, Libra, or Aquarius). If your natal sun sign is a social air sign, your progressed sun will move into an emotional water sign (Cancer, Scorpio, or Pisces). If your natal sun sign is an emotional water sign, your progressed sun will move into a spirited fire sign (Aries, Leo, or Sagittarius).

Thus throughout one's lifetime, every person at some time takes on a temperament different from one's natal sun sign, while still retaining the original nature. This will happen about three times during your life span. Human nature is complex and changing, yet complex and changing according to pattern.

The progressed sun sign is always based on the date that is as many days after your birth date as is your age in years. Consult the following tables to pinpoint your sun's progressions. The progressed sun sign in the tables will be designated as PSS. As you find your progressed sun sign, read its characteristics. They will show the changing influences that result from the sun's apparent move through the zodiac after your birth.

The sun does not enter the next sign on the same day every year. Therefore, in the following tables the numerals at the end or the beginning of a sun sign period may overlap. If your birthday is the last day or the first day of a sun sign period, it is well to determine your sun sign accurately. This may be done by consulting an ephemeris, which is a book with the sun, moon, and planet placements for every day of any year. Or you may obtain a computer printout of your individual birth chart showing the precise positions of the sun, moon, and planets at the time of your birth. A birth chart may be ordered at nominal cost from the advertisers or the editorial department of most astrology magazines which are sold at news stands. However, the following tables will suffice for most birth dates.

The tables will deal with each of the twelve sun signs, telling you at what age your progressed sun enters another sign. This information will reveal to you another intriguing facet of your personality. It will be a prediction of your future development.

Aries

If you are an Aries born on March 21, your progressed sun sign will enter Taurus as you reach about age 31. It will move into Gemini at about age 61, and into Cancer at about age 92 if you are fortunate to live that long. Consult the table below for other Aries birth dates.

If you were born on	PSS enters Taurus at age	PSS enters Gemini at age	PSS enters Cancer at age
Mar 21	31	61	92
22	30	60	91
23	29	59	90
24	28	58	89
25	27	57	88
26	26	56	87
27	25	55	86
28	24	54	85
29	23	53	84
30	22	52	83
31	21	51	82
Apr 1	20	50	81
2	19	49	80
3	18	48	79
4	17	47	78
5	16	46	77
6	15	45	76
7	14	44	75
8	13	43	74
9	12	42	73
10	11	41	72
11	10	40	71
12	9	39	70
13	8	38	69
14	7	37	68
15	6	36	67
16	5	35	66
17	4	34	65
18	3	33	64
19	2	32	63
20	1	31	62

Taurus

If you are a Taurus born on April 21, your progressed sun sign will enter Gemini as you reach about age 30. It will move into Cancer at about age 61, and into Leo at about age 91 if you are fortunate to live that long. Consult the table below for other Taurus birth dates.

If you were born on	PSS enters Gemini at age	PSS enters Cancer at age	PSS enters Leo at age
Apr 21	30	61	91
22	29	60	90
23	28	59	89
24	27	58	88
25	26	57	87
26	25	56	86
27	24	55	85
28	23	54	84
29	22	53	83
30	21	52	82
May 1	20	51	81
2	19	50	80
3	18	49	79
4	17	48	78
5	16	47	77
6	15	46	76
7	14	45	75
8	13	44	74
9	12	43	73
10	11	42	72
11	10	41	71
12	9	40	70
13	8	39	69
14	7	38	68
15	6	37	67
16	5	36	66
17	4	35	65
18	3	34	64
19	2	33	63
20	1	32	62

Gemini

If you are a Gemini born on May 21, your progressed sun sign will enter Cancer as you reach about age 31. It will move into Leo at about age 61, and into Virgo at about age 91 if you are fortunate to live that long. Consult the table below for other Gemini birth dates.

If you were born on	PSS enters Cancer at age	PSS enters Leo at age	PSS enters Virgo at age
May 21	31	61	91
22	30	60	90
23	29	59	89
24	28	58	88
25	27	57	87
26	26	56	86
27	25	55	85
28	24	54	84
29	23	53	83
30	22	52	82
31	21	51	81
June 1	20	50	80
2	19	49	79
3	18	48	78
4	17	47	77
5	16	46	76
6	15	45	75
7	14	44	74
8	13	43	73
9	12	42	72
10	11	41	71
11	10	40	70
12	9	39	69
13	8	38	68
14	7	37	67
15	6	36	66
16	5	35	65
17	4	34	64
18	3	33	63
19	2	32	62
20	1	31	61

Cancer

If you are a Cancer born on June 22, your progressed sun sign will enter Leo as you reach about age 30. It will move into Virgo at about age 61, and into Libra at about age 92 if you are fortunate to live that long. Consult the table below for other Cancer birth dates.

If you were born on	PSS enters Leo at age	PSS enters Virgo at age	PSS enters Libra at age
June 21	31	62	93
22	30	61	92
23	29	60	91
24	28	59	90
25	27	58	89
26	26	57	88
27	25	56	87
28	24	55	86
29	23	54	85
30	22	53	84
July 1	21	52	83
2	20	51	82
3	19	50	81
4	18	49	80
5	17	48	79
6	16	47	78
7	15	46	77
8	14	45	76
9	13	44	75
10	12	43	74
11	11	42	73
12	10	41	72
13	9	40	71
14	8	39	70
15	7	38	69
16	6	37	68
17	5	36	67
18	4	35	66
19	3	34	65
20	2	33	64
21	1	32	63

Leo

If you are a Leo born on July 22, your progressed sun sign will enter Virgo as you reach about age 32. It will move into Libra at about age 63, and into Scorpio at about age 93. Consult the table below for other Leo birth dates.

If you were born on	PSS enters Virgo at age	PSS enters Libra at age	PSS enters Scorpio at age
July 22	32	63	93
23	31	62	92
24	30	61	91
25	29	60	90
26	28	59	89
27	27	58	88
28	26	57	87
29	25	56	86
30	24	55	85
31	23	54	84
Aug 1	22	53	83
2	21	52	82
3	20	51	81
4	19	50	80
5	18	49	79
6	17	48	78
7	16	47	77
8	15	46	76
9	14	45	75
10	13	44	74
11	12	43	73
12	11	42	72
13	10	41	71
14	9	40	70
15	8	39	69
16	7	38	68
17	6	37	67
18	5	36	66
19	4	35	65
20	3	34	64
21	2	33	63
22	1	32	62

Virgo

If you are a Virgo born on August 23, your progressed sun sign will enter Libra as you reach about age 31. It will move into Scorpio at about age 61, and into Sagittarius at about age 92. Consult the table below for other Virgo birth dates.

If you were born on	PSS enters Libra at age	PSS enters Scorpio at age	PSS enters Sagittarius at age
Aug 23	31	61	92
24	30	60	91
25	29	59	90
26	28	58	89
27	27	57	88
28	26	56	87
29	25	55	86
30	24	54	85
31	23	53	84
Sept 1	22	52	83
2	21	51	82
3	20	50	81
4	19	49	80
5	18	48	79
6	17	47	78
7	16	46	77
8	15	45	76
9	14	44	75
10	13	43	74
11	12	42	73
12	11	41	72
13	10	40	71
14	9	39	70
15	8	38	69
16	7	37	68
17	6	36	67
18	5	35	66
19	4	34	65
20	3	33	64
21	2	32	63
22	1	31	62

Libra

If you are a Libra born on September 23, your progressed sun sign will enter Scorpio as you reach about age 30. It will move into Sagittarius at about age 60, and into Capricorn at about age 90. Consult the table below for other Libra birth dates.

If you were born on	PSS enters Scorpio at age	PSS enters Sagittarius at age	PSS enters Capricorn at age
Sept 23	30	60	90
24	29	59	89
25	28	58	88
26	27	57	87
27	26	56	86
28	25	55	85
29	24	54	84
30	23	53	83
Oct 1	22	52	82
2	21	51	81
3	20	50	80
4	19	49	79
5	18	48	78
6	17	47	77
7	16	46	76
8	15	45	75
9	14	44	74
10	13	43	73
11	12	42	72
12	11	41	71
13	10	40	70
14	9	39	69
15	8	38	68
16	7	37	67
17	6	36	66
18	5	35	65
19	4	34	64
20	3	33	63
21	2	32	62
22	1	31	61

Scorpio

If you are a Scorpio born on October 23, your progressed sun sign will enter Sagittarius as you reach about age 31. It will move into Capricorn at about age 60, and into Aquarius at about age 90. Consult the table below for other Scorpio birth dates.

If you were born on	PSS enters Sagittarius at age	PSS enters Capricorn at age	PSS Enters Aquarius at age
Oct 23	31	60	90
24	30	59	89
25	29	58	88
26	28	57	87
27	27	56	86
28	26	55	85
29	25	54	84
30	24	53	83
31	23	52	82
Nov 1	22	51	81
2	21	50	80
3	20	49	79
4	19	48	78
5	18	47	77
6	17	46	76
7	16	45	75
8	15	44	74
9	14	43	73
10	13	42	72
11	12	41	71
12	11	40	70
13	10	39	69
14	9	38	68
15	8	37	67
16	7	36	66
17	6	35	65
18	5	34	64
19	4	33	63
20	3	32	62
21	2	31	61
22	1	30	60

Sagittarius

If you are a Sagittarius born on November 23, your progressed sun sign will enter Capricorn as you reach about age 30. It will move into Aquarius at about age 60, and into Pisces at about age 89. Consult the table below for other Sagittarius birth dates.

If you were born on	PSS enters Capricorn at age	PSS enters Aquarius at age	PSS enters Pisces at age
Nov 23	30	60	89
24	29	59	88
25	28	58	87
26	27	57	86
27	26	56	85
28	25	55	84
29	24	54	83
30	23	53	82
Dec 1	22	52	81
2	21	51	80
3	20	50	79
4	19	49	78
5	18	48	77
6	17	47	76
7	16	46	75
8	15	45	74
9	14	44	73
10	13	43	72
11	12	42	71
12	11	41	70
13	10	40	69
14	9	39	68
15	8	38	67
16	7	37	66
17	6	36	65
18	5	35	64
19	4	34	63
20	3	33	62
21	2	32	61
22	1	31	60

Capricorn

If you are a Capricorn born on December 23, your progressed sun sign will enter Aquarius as you reach about age 29. It will move into Pisces at about age 59, and into Aries at about age 89. Consult the table below for other Capricorn birth dates.

If you were born on	PSS enters Aquarius at age	PSS enters Pisces at age	PSS enters Aries at age
Dec 23	29	59	89
24	28	58	88
25	27	57	87
26	26	56	86
27	25	55	85
28	24	54	84
29	23	53	83
30	22	52	82
31	21	51	81
Jan 1	20	50	80
2	19	49	79
3	18	48	78
4	17	47	77
5	16	46	76
6	15	45	75
7	14	44	74
8	13	43	73
9	12	42	72
10	11	41	71
11	10	40	70
12	9	39	69
13	8	38	68
14	7	37	67
15	6	36	66
16	5	35	65
17	4	34	64
18	3	33	63
19	2	32	62
20	1	31	61

Aquarius

If you are an Aquarius born on January 21, your progressed sun sign will enter Pisces as you reach about age 30. It will move into Aries at about age 60, and into Taurus at about age 90. Consult the table below for other Aquarius birth dates

If you were born on	PSS enters Pisces at age	PSS enters Aries at age	PSS enters Taurus at age
Jan 21	30	60	90
22	29	59	89
23	28	58	88
24	27	57	87
25	26	56	86
26	25	55	85
27	24	54	84
28	23	53	83
29	22	52	82
30	21	51	81
31	20	50	80
Feb 1	19	49	79
2	18	48	78
3	17	47	77
4	16	46	76
5	15	45	75
6	14	44	74
7	13	43	73
8	12	42	72
9	11	41	71
10	10	40	70
11	9	39	69
12	8	38	68
13	7	37	67
14	6	36	66
15	5	35	65
16	4	34	64
17	3	33	63
18	2	32	62
19	1	31	61

Pisces

If you are a Pisces born on February 20, your progressed sun sign will enter Aries as you reach about age 30. It will move into Taurus at about age 60, and into Gemini at about age 91. Consult the table below for other Pisces birthdates.

If you were born on	PSS enters Aries at age	PSS enters Taurus at age	PSS enters Gemini at age
Feb 20	30	60	91
21	29	59	90
22	28	58	89
23	27	57	88
24	26	56	87
25	25	55	86
26	24	54	85
27	23	53	84
28	22	52	83
Mar 1	21	51	82
2	20	50	81
3	19	49	80
4	18	48	79
5	17	47	78
6	16	46	77
7	15	45	76
8	14	44	75
9	13	43	74
10	12	42	73
11	11	41	72
12	10	40	71
13	9	39	70
14	8	38	69
15	7	37	68
16	6	36	67
17	5	35	66
18	4	34	65
19	3	33	64
20	2	32	63
21	1	31	62

NOTES

NOTES

NOTES

NOTES

NOTES

NOTES

NOTES

NOTES

NOTES

NOTES